Philip Stafford Moxom

The Religion of Hope

Philip Stafford Moxom

The Religion of Hope

ISBN/EAN: 9783337088132

Printed in Europe, USA, Canada, Australia, Japan

Cover: Foto ©Lupo / pixelio.de

More available books at **www.hansebooks.com**

THE RELIGION OF HOPE

THE
RELIGION OF HOPE

BY

PHILIP STAFFORD MOXOM

AUTHOR OF

"THE AIM OF LIFE," AND "FROM JERUSALEM TO NICÆA"

BOSTON
ROBERTS BROTHERS
1896

Copyright, 1895,
BY ROBERTS BROTHERS.

University Press:
JOHN WILSON AND SON, CAMBRIDGE, U.S.A.

TO

MY WIFE AND CHILDREN.

PREFACE.

THE sermons contained in this volume were not composed with reference to any unity of plan. They have been selected from the accumulated product of thirteen years of labor. The earliest was written in 1880, the latest in 1893. All were preached during my ministry of eight and a half years in Boston, and all but two were written in that period. All, of course, have been subjected to revision, but not to such revision as to change their essential form and substance. Thus they truly reflect the attitude of my mind and heart toward the fundamental truths of Christianity during the larger part of my service as a Christian minister; and they show that the note of hopefulness has been, throughout, a dominant note. In arranging these sermons for publication, I have not followed the chronological order, but rather have sought to put them in something like a logical sequence. They begin with hope, and end with heaven. A considerable number have been printed in periodicals, one of them two or three times. They are now presented to the public in permanent form mainly in response to many requests both of former parishioners and of others, and with the earnest wish that they may bear a heartening message to some of those who have found, or would find, in the Christian hope the great solace for their afflictions and the unwasting inspiration for their endeavors.

PHILIP STAFFORD MOXOM.

WINGOOD LODGE, SPRINGFIELD, MASS.,
December, 1895.

CONTENTS.

		PAGE
I.	CHRISTIANITY THE RELIGION OF HOPE	13
II.	THE LOVE OF GOD	37
III.	THE KINGDOM OF GOD	55
IV.	THE COMING OF CHRIST	75
V.	SAVING OTHERS AND SAVING SELF	93
VI.	THE MIND OF CHRIST	113
VII.	THE ENTHUSIASM OF JESUS	133
VIII.	CHRISTIAN UNITY	151
IX.	THE CHURCH, THE BODY OF CHRIST	169
X.	THE INCREASE FROM GOD	187
XI.	FORSAKING ALL FOR CHRIST	203
XII.	A QUESTION OF THE HEART	221
XIII.	FOES IN THE HOUSEHOLD	243
XIV.	NOT DESTRUCTION BUT FULFILMENT	261
XV.	THE JOY OF THE LORD	277
XVI.	THE NEED OF PATIENCE	297
XVII.	THE WAY TO HEAVEN	315

I.

CHRISTIANITY THE RELIGION OF HOPE.

My own hope is, a sun will pierce
   The thickest cloud earth ever stretched:
That, after Last, returns the First,
   Though a wide compass round be fetched;
That what began best, can't end worst,
   Nor what God blessed once, prove accurst.
                              ROBERT BROWNING.

THE RELIGION OF HOPE.

I.

CHRISTIANITY THE RELIGION OF HOPE.

Now the God of hope fill you with all joy and peace in believing, that ye may abound in hope, in the power of the Holy Spirit. — ROM. xv. 13.

CHRISTIANITY is pre-eminently the religion of hope. Its chief message to the world is the declaration of God's good-will toward men, and its chief expression is Jesus of Nazareth, whom God anointed "with the Holy Spirit and with power; who went about doing good, and healing all that were oppressed of the devil; for God was with him."

In forming our judgment of Christianity, we must discriminate between what is accidental and transient on the one hand, and what is essential and permanent on the other. The discriminating process must be carried, not only through all the organizations and institutions and theories and history that are generally designated by the term "Christian," but also through the Scriptures of the Old and New Testaments. In these Scriptures we find a revelation of God which surpasses all others in clearness and fulness. This is not the only revelation of God, for there are also divine revelations in the order of nature, and in the constitution and history of man. These, from one point of view, are preparatory, logically, if not always chronologically, for the revelation in the Bible; from another point of view, they both supplement and confirm that revelation. By virtue of his spiritual nature, man has a capacity for knowing God, and to this capacity there has always been a corresponding communication. Were it not for the subjective capacity, there could be no objective revelation.

The Biblical revelation is historical and progressive, exhibiting a distinct advance from the naïve monotheism of Abraham and Moses, with its predominant anthropomorphic elements, to the purer and loftier monotheism of the eighth century prophets; and there is a still greater advance from the monotheism of the prophets to the profound spiritual theism of Jesus.

Because revelation is progressive, corresponding to man's growing power of apprehension, and depending upon it, there are many features of the revelatory process that are incidental and transient. Learning is, in part, a process of discarding. Low ideas of the divine nature are continually replaced by higher. New points of view necessitate an abandonment of the old. Imperfect symbols are dropped, as their defects become apparent, and better symbols take their place. For example, as I have suggested, the later prophets, — Micah, the two Isaiahs, Jeremiah, and others, — in their conception of the Deity, show great progress beyond the conception which was attained even by the best minds of the times of the Exodus and the Judges, or even by the earlier prophets, — Samuel, Elijah, and Elisha; while Jesus occupies a far higher level of spiritual view than that of the prophets, and his thought has a larger spiritual content than theirs.

This progress is not in any sense artificial, nor is it a mere order of sequence; it is vital and experimental, and has an indestructible continuity. In the advance much is left behind, but something is steadily carried forward. The new is, in a true sense, the out-growth of the old. The plant is the evolution of the seed, but the process of development is also a process of incrementation.

In order, therefore, to get a true and adequate idea of the Biblical revelation of God, we must take our stand on the highest point reached in the revelatory process which has record in the Bible, and that is the personality and teachings of Jesus Christ. From this point we may trace the slowly ascending and slowly brightening path that leads up from the Mosaic age to the time when Jesus, comprehending at once the essential nature of God and the manner and form in which that nature is most perfectly revealed to man, said: "God is spirit," and "He that hath seen me hath seen the Father." Manifestly, to take our position at any point in the process of Biblical revelation short of the summit on which Jesus stands, and to say of the view obtainable from that point, "This is the true vision of God," is to misunderstand and to misrepresent the Bible.

The same is true with respect to the idea of Christianity which we are to derive from the record of the revelation that rises to culminating expression in the Son of God. No book of the Bible, preceding the Gospels, truly represents or defines Christianity. Only in Him of whose spirit Christianity is the effluence do we find a true exponent of what essential Christianity is.

But there is also a prophetic element in the Biblical revelation of God. What Jesus gives to the world is not simply another and higher stage in the revelatory process than that which is given successively by patriarchs and prophets. The singularity of his communication is partly in this, that his revelation of the Father is not only complementary to all preceding revelation, but it is also prophetic and ideal. The value of the New Testament is chiefly in the fact that it is far more than a high-water mark of the generic spiritual perception of men. It sets a standard toward which the world still strives, and communicates a thought which the world has not yet wholly grasped. The spiritual progress of so much of humanity as has come within the circle of Biblical communication is a progress, not beyond the point reached in the New Testament, but toward that point, that prophetic revelation which Jesus, the chiefest of all the prophets, or speakers for God, both gave and was. All the advance of philosophical thought toward the true and perfect idea of God has been an advance toward the thought of Jesus. All the progress of that spiritual life which is the expression of spiritual thought is a progress toward the life of Him who "came from God and went to God," the "Son of Man," who was yet "the only begotten Son of God."

So, too, and necessarily, there is a prophetic and ideal element in the idea of Christianity which Jesus gives. The religious thought and life of to-day are far higher and purer than the religious thought and life of the early Christian centuries. This is a truth which no careful student of Christian history will for a moment deny. Both the intellectual apprehension and the practical application of Christian principles are broader and juster and more thoroughgoing to-day than at any time in the past. Yet, when we succeed in clearly discriminating essential Christianity from all that is incidental and adventitious; when we carry this process not only through historical and institutional Christianity, but even through the New Testament, until we discover the fundamental and enduring elements of the Christianity which Jesus embodied in his person and manifested in his action and expressed in his authenticated teachings, — we can understand the real meaning of Lessing's extravagant, yet not altogether untrue saying: " The religion of Christianity has been on trial eighteen hundred years; the religion of Christ is yet to be tried." We shall understand also, and approve, the statement of Principal Fairbairn, that true Christianity "is an ideal for the whole of humanity, and a great method for its realization."

The revelation which Jesus makes of the divine interest in man, and the divine purpose to be realized in man, discloses also the forces and motives by which man is to achieve a spiritual destiny in the unfolding of the kingdom of God. The fundamental element in the Christianity of Jesus is the love of God for humanity. This love lies at the base of all supernatural manifestations, is the law of all providential discipline, the spring of all ethics, and the ground of all hopes. No communication takes rank with this communication. No principle limits or conditions this principle. As high as heaven, as deep as hell, as wide as space, is this fact which Jesus utters and embodies, — the love of God for men. Essential Christianity is the declaration and concrete expression of this love through the archetypal divine sonship and self-sacrifice of Jesus. All the forces that work for human salvation, in the widest sense, flow out of this elemental fact thus expressed in a unique yet universally related and all-relating personality. The revelation which Jesus makes of divine Fatherhood and human sonship discloses the ideal toward the full realization of which the moral and spiritual life of man is a progress. This divine-human relation involves in itself the perfect good of the individual man and the perfect good of mankind. On the fundamental fact of man's moral relation to God, a relation exhibited and confirmed by the Christ, rests every principle, and out of it rises every force of that great upward movement of humanity to which history, with increasing clearness, bears witness. All that is best in our individual characters, as well as in our social morals, our sciences, arts, industries, politics, and religions, has its primal spring in that relation. Ignorant as he may be blind and bestial as he often is, man nevertheless is the child of God; therefore he is the object of the divine love, the subject of the divine tuition and discipline, and, in the attainment of his true destiny, the fulfilment of the divine purpose. The revelation of God's attitude toward man and of man's true relation to God, which Jesus makes, involves all that is essential in his teaching and in his experience. It involves the cross, not as a necessary material fact, but as a symbol of spiritual fact, — the fact of supreme self-sacrifice for moral ends.

There is much of form and organization and theory that has got itself named Christian, which, at the best, sustains but a loose and accidental relation to essential Christianity. There is much also which essential Christianity has created as instrument for the realization of its ends. All this, for the present, may be left aside. Nor is it necessary here to attempt a detailed elucidation of the spiritual contents of essential Christianity, either as doctrine or as life. A single point now claims attention. Christianity as a revelation of divine Fatherhood and human sonship, and of divine love seeking the full realization of truth and love in human experience and character and destiny, is pre-eminently a religion of hope.

In a higher degree than ever any other teacher personally represented what he taught, Jesus personally represented and embodied essential Christianity. It never should be forgotten that Christianity is fundamentally a spirit and method of life. It is not primarily a church, nor a ritual, nor a theology, nor even a religion, but a life from God and in God, which has its supreme embodiment in Jesus Christ. It is far more than a system of ethics or an ethical regimen. As far as mere ethical principles are concerned, there is little in it that is original; though the moment we consider the question of moral motives, the originality of

Jesus' method vividly appears. It is difficult, if not impossible, to find any precept in the Gospels which, in some form, had not been given to men before. Indeed, the great doctrines of the unity of God, the Divine Providence over earthly affairs, the Fatherhood of God, the ubiquity of the Divine Spirit, the mercifulness of God to sinners, man's duty of repentance and faith toward God and charity toward his fellow-man, and the hope of immortality, all had found expression in some form before Jesus came. But the full significance of truth expressed in a life the world had not seen until Jesus came. What men had apprehended only in detached fragments of spiritual truth and beauty, and, for the most part, in the form of precept or proposition, Jesus exhibited in the harmony and completeness of a living embodiment. Thus embodied, all truths took on a new meaning, or rather, now first disclosed their real meaning. To see one who loved God with all his heart and soul and mind and strength, and his neighbor as himself, made the old precept a new communication. To see in the clear face of the Son the unmarred reflection of the perfect Father made the revelation of God a new revelation. To see faith and obedience and holy love perfectly realized in a human life was to have a new sense of what faith and obedience and love are. In Jesus all the scattered rays of truth were gathered up into the glowing and dynamic centre of a divinely human personality. He justified, therefore, as well as inspired, the testimony that, "God having of old time spoken unto the fathers in the prophets by divers portions and in divers manners, hath at the end of these days spoken unto us in a Son."

Jesus Christ, then, in his person and teaching and deeds, is the Gospel,— the good tidings of God to men. His function, as well as his person, is thus, in a true sense, unique. Neither prophet nor apostle, neither Isaiah nor Paul, but Jesus only, adequately expresses and defines essential Christianity. The real progress of Christian thought is advance in power to understand and interpret Jesus. A book may be exhausted, for the capacity of "the letter" is limited; but a personality — such a personality — is inexhaustible. "The letter" is form, and easily becomes fetters; "the spirit" is life, and has no bounds. Men are perpetually trying to put Christianity into dogmatic systems, which they label Calvinism and Arminianism, Old Theology and New Theology; but they are perpetually baffled by the fact that Christianity, as the effluence of the living Christ, overflows all boundaries, transcends all forms, and convicts all definitions of inadequacy and error. Everything is transitory save the spirit. Jesus, as the revelation of God and the manifestation of the love of God realized and individualized in the spirit of man, is the secret of the power which

Christianity possesses of perpetually renewing itself. Institutions, theories, and forms become decadent and effete. Then men say, Christianity is moribund; but while they are brooding over the death of a faith, behold! that faith is rising in fresh power, putting forth new energies and creating new instruments to serve its ends.

A clear apprehension of Christianity as a spirit of life, having its supreme manifestation in the Son of God, makes argument to prove that it is a religion of hope seem almost superfluous.

But let us proceed to explicate this truth somewhat in detail. The message of Jesus to the world was one of hope, for it was a message of salvation. He declared that "God so loved the world that he gave his only begotten Son, that whosoever trusteth in him might not perish but have life eternal," and he presented himself as the expression of this love and the executor of this purpose. He took to himself, as definitive of his mission, in a broader sense than the prophet understood, the words of the Isaiah of the exile:

"The Spirit of the Lord is upon me,
 Because he anointed me to preach good tidings to the poor:
 He has sent me to proclaim release to the captives,
 And recovering of sight to the blind,
 To set at liberty them that are bruised,
 To proclaim the acceptable year of the Lord."

He came not to rebuke men, but to enlighten them. His message was one of cheer, not one of condemnation: "For God sent not the Son into the world to judge the world; but that the world should be saved through him." His words were continually provocative of hope. His ministry of healing was, in a large, sweet way, illustrative and symbolical. His practical helpfulness reinforced his declarations of divine purpose in a manner that men could feel and understand. From the earliest times men were more ready to credit God with the purpose of smiting than they were to believe in his disposition to heal. Jesus declared the love of God to men, and, avowedly fulfilling the will of God, put the message into a palpable gift of health to diseased and tormented bodies. Thus he dissolved that ignorant fear of God which was a main hindrance to the reception of his message. He declared the law of love between man and man, and illustrated the declaration by his invincible goodness and his utter unselfishness in helping the needy of every class. Thus he dissolved the antagonisms that thrust men apart and made them mutual hurters instead of mutual helpers of one another. He uttered and embodied the divine principle of love which is at once the motive of true worship and the law of right action. This was lifting life to a new level. His purpose was but dimly apprehended then, and is far from being clearly apprehended even now. Still, despite their little apprehension of Jesus, many of those among whom he lived and taught awoke to a new hope, and the impulse of that hope created the new life which dates from the resurrection of Jesus.

What Jesus did, he does still. The material circumstances of his ministry, for example, his works of healing, as to their form, are incidental. In essence, the ministry of Jesus continues; and not as the prolonged impression of historic events simply, but as the ever fresh impression of his spiritual force — his transcendent personality. Treating his life historically, we must say "he was," and "he did"; but treating his life on the higher plane of his essential mission to the world, we instinctively drop the past tense. The Christ belongs to all time, and is the contemporary of every age. His message is not a mere reminiscence of a past event; it is a vital communication of the present and dateless gospel of God.

The world has greatly changed in the nearly two millenniums that have passed since Jesus of Nazareth began his ministry in Palestine, but it has not lost its essential relation to him. He is more familiar to the general mind, but he is still pre-eminent. His teaching is better understood, but its force is still unexhausted. Man is less abject and bestial, less ignorant and superstitious than he was, but he is still dependent upon "our Lord and Saviour Jesus Christ." In a true sense, then, what Jesus did, he still does; only, the scope of his ministry ever widens as man's capacity to understand and appreciate that ministry increases.

Jesus' message of hope to men was not simply a promise of "something better by and by,"—that is, in eternity, conceived as a condition of being to be entered upon by mankind collectively at the end of time. He did not say, "Life is evil and irremediable here and now, but in the hereafter it will be wholly good." He had little to say of the hereafter, in the sense in which that term is commonly used. He said enough. He gave the fruitful germs of thought that grow with the growth of man's spirit into ever enlarging spiritual conceptions of humanity's future. But he did not speak as fully and as explicitly of the hereafter as many have supposed. The promise of "the better by and by" which men needed to hear was implicitly in all his teaching, but the pledge of its fulfilment was to be found in a bettered present. If the seed of the better age is not in to-day, its flower and fruit will not appear in the distant to-morrow. Jesus did not leave men in their misery simply enriched by a hope. He began in their minds and hearts the process which, making the present better, brightens all the future. Man himself must be improved if there is to be any permanent improvement of his environment. Civilization is first subjective. Jesus gave to men a revelation of God that awakened trust in the divine goodness. This trust was itself at once a ground and spring of hope and a powerful motive to righteousness. To deepen one's faith in the good is to generate rational hope and to elevate character. He taught men the meaning of love and planted in them the root of that divine affection which must grow from heart to heart until all humanity is bound in indissoluble, holy brotherhood. The man who loves to-day, even feebly, gives promise in himself of the day when men will love their neighbors as themselves. What Jesus did *for* man was, most of all, what he did *in* man, and in man he began the process of which "the new heaven and the new earth" will be the natural and divinely ordained culmination. The leaven in the meal is the finest symbol of Christ's method. The spirit works within, and from within outward.

The character of Jesus' work in man is the best answer to the pessimism of much "Christian theology," as well as of unchristian philosophy. He gave to human life an impulse toward the good that strengthens and broadens with every passing century. In giving that impulse he discloses at once both the actual and the ideal of human life from the moral point of view. What life is, he shows less by any denunciation of evil than by the light which he sheds upon it from the height of his own excellence. His pure spirit inevitably reveals and condemns the grossness and sordidness of men. His utter truth exposes and judges their deep insincerities. His absolute goodness unmasks and rebukes their multiform selfishness. No words can represent the deformities and deficiencies of man's life from a moral point of view so vividly as those appear in the light of Jesus' character. This disclosure of the actual he made, and this disclosure he still makes. To-day, as truly as when he walked in Judea, he lays bare the sin and folly of men. Uttering no audible word, he stands in our market-places and shows the immoralities and selfishness of our trade; he stands in our churches and uncovers our miserable insincerities and slavish idolatries. When we look at him with honest, open eyes, our conceit shrivels, and our petty proprieties and conventional moralities refuse longer to hide from us our real defects and positive sins. This disclosure Jesus inevitably makes, because in him is the reality of truth and righteousness.

But while he thus discloses the actual, he also discloses the possible, — the ideal. What he is in spirit shows men what they may be. His stainless purity, his boundless charity, his invulnerable sweetness and patience, his unbroken, intimate communion with the Father, his loftiness of mind, his perfect righteousness, his wonderful peace — that peace which we so admire and covet and yet so piteously fail to attain — that peace which, when every one else was torn by passion, or fretted by care, or shaken by fear, or harassed by doubt, enveloped him in an atmosphere of beautiful holy calm, — all this reveals to us our possible attainments as children of God. This disclosure to us of human excellence kindles hope in our hearts, and hope passes into aspiration and impulse. " Looking unto Jesus " becomes a striving toward "the perfect man, . . . the measure of the stature of the fulness of Christ." All spiritual progress in the individual life witnesses to the presence and illustrates the power of the hope that Jesus awakens.

But the ideal disclosed is more than an ideal of individual life. There is a great prophetical suggestiveness in the life and teaching of Jesus. In himself he prophesies, not only the coming man, but also the coming order, the coming reign of love, the coming health of the world, and the coming peace. The ideal is not sharply defined in words. It is hinted, rather, and the hints, at first vague, grow clearer and clearer with the growth of men in power to see and to lay hold of the spiritual meaning and ends of life. Explicitly, Jesus did speak of the kingdom of God; but the conception was too great to be grasped at once, as it is too expansive to be exhausted at any point in subsequent history. But it was definite enough to constitute an ideal grand and sweet, if vague; and from that ideal sprang the hope which works perpetually toward a higher civic and economic organization of human society, and purer government, and larger liberty.

So, in this twofold disclosure of the actual and the ideal, Jesus begets hope in man's heart. Indeed, the very disclosure of the actual and the possible, in connection with each other, generates in man the unquenchable desire to pass from the one to the other. Hope is the reaching forward of the soul from the actual to the ideal. St. Paul significantly said: "We are saved by hope."

But the self-revelation which Jesus gives, — the exhibition of himself as the Son of Man and the Son of God, — in his function of lover and Saviour of the world, is central, because the highest power among men is personal. It is not the touch of precepts or ideas or theories, but the touch of a personality, that moves us, that imparts the vital impulse. The love of Christ, the love which he wakens in our hearts, is the great spring of hope, because that love makes us sharers in his aspirations, his ideals, his faith, and his enterprise. That love binds us to him in his entire mission. Amidst a world seemingly tottering to its ruin, he stood and *saw* the salvation of the world and the triumph of good — saw it through the shadow of the cross that fell darkly athwart his path. Surrendering himself to the sharpness and apparent utter defeat of death, even while dying he triumphed in the vision of a completed redemption. Loving him, man shares in his power of forecast and triumphant anticipation. Under the influence of this transcendent personality, man strives to realize in himself and in the world the ends toward which Jesus wrought, and so becomes missionary and martyr of the gospel. Hope passes from a sentiment into a principle. It incorporates itself into character. It becomes an element of righteousness because it is rooted in the soul's faith in God, and conviction of the reality and permanence of the good.

This hope, which Jesus awakens and continually nourishes, is the pledge of the salvation of the world. It is a spring of spiritual energy beneath all our Christian institutions and organizations; and, vitalizing missionary enterprise, transforms it from a perfunctory or selfish propagandism into a confident and enthusiastic service of love to humanity. Often repudiated in theories of human life, and denied in the actions of men, and dishonored by feeble utterances in the creeds of the church, it persists in all hearts that Jesus has touched and quickened into the life of the spirit. In some form it is the real force of human progress. It is the silent but most true witness to the divinity that shapes the course of human history, and to the divine origin and immortality of the human soul. In "the hope of the gospel," that gospel which Jesus embodies and perpetually imparts, the salvation of the world is already prophetically achieved; and the Christian sings with a victor's confidence: —

> "I feel the earth move sunward,
> I join the great march onward,
> And take by faith while living
> My freehold of thanksgiving."

Hope, then, is not a matter of mere sentiment, or of a happy temperament. It is allied, not with weakness, but with strength; not with baseless speculation, but with firm grasp of fundamental truth; not with fond and foolish fancy, but with solidest loyalty to righteousness; not with easy credulousness, but with most strenuous and most reasonable faith in God. To hope for the final and absolute supremacy of goodness is among the finest and most rational exercises of Christian virtue. It is doubt that is weakness; it is pessimism that is the real denial of the Christian faith. It is want of large, tenacious, and invincible hope that often turns the nominal Church of Christ into a half-hearted army, feebly fighting a battle of which defeat is a foregone and accepted conclusion.

To cultivate hopefulness is a duty, quite as much as it is a duty to cultivate morality. It belongs to the Christian's discipline in righteousness. Rational optimism, the optimism of the Christian faith and the Christian spirit, is grounded in the reality and perfection of God. It is the irrefutable deduction from the gospel of the Son of God, which is the gospel of Sovereign Law and Sovereign Love.

"The truths of God forever shine,
  Though error glare and falsehood rage;
The Cause of Order is divine,
  And Wisdom rules from age to age.

"Faith, Hope, and Love, your time abide!
  Let Hades marshal all his hosts,
The heavenly forces with you side,
  The stars are watching at their posts."

II.

THE LOVE OF GOD.

DOUBT no longer that the Highest is the wisest and the best,
Let not all that saddens Nature blight thy hope or break thy rest,
Quail not at the fiery mountain, at the shipwreck, or the rolling
Thunder, or the rending earthquake, or the famine, or the pest!
Neither mourn if human creeds be lower than the heart's desire!
Thro' the gates that bar the distance comes a gleam of what is higher.
Wait till Death has flung them open, when the man will make the Maker
Dark no more with human hatreds in the glare of deathless fire!

         ALFRED TENNYSON.

II.

THE LOVE OF GOD.

God is love. — 1 JOHN iv. 16.

God so loved the world that he gave his only begotten Son, that whosoever believeth in him should not perish, but have eternal life. — JOHN iii. 16.

THESE two sentences express one truth, and that truth is the chief revelation in the sacred Scriptures. It is at once the reason and cause and the supreme motive of the Christian ministry. "God is love," and "God so loved the world," — that is revelation. Not all the Bible is revelation; not all the New Testament, even, is revelation; but this is a disclosure of the very mind and heart of God. Jesus gave it to us. John the Apostle *said* it, but Jesus *lived* it, and *was* it. Every other text of Scripture is a fragment, as an arc is a fragment of a circle; but this text sweeps the perfect round. There is in it more of God's infinity than there is in any other. The dullest mind must feel something of its illimitable suggestion. It gives one a deeper sense of infinite room and glory than even Wordsworth felt when greeted by some one with the words, "What, you are stepping westward?" in the splendor of a sunset by Loch Katrine: —

> "I liked the greeting; 't was a sound
> Of something without place or bound;
> And seemed to give me spiritual right
> To travel through that region bright."

Christianity has its root and reason of being in this truth, that God is love, and God loved the world. This is its cardinal article of faith. Whatever conditions or limitations have been put upon this revelation by the narrow thought and sympathies of men, and whatever contradictions of it have found place in theology, belong not to truth but to error. The worst heterodoxy is that which attempts, theoretically or practically, to lessen the breadth and force of this great communication, "God is love." This sentence, this truth in its simple grandeur, is the ground of every sweet and reasonable hope that can come to the heart of man; in this truth is the solvent of every difficulty in the dark problem of human life. To receive this revelation, to believe and in some measure understand it, and to be inspired, uplifted, and transformed by its power, is to become truly Christian.

It is difficult to speak of the love of God, partly because it is so great and wonderful: speech is inadequate, and one is ashamed to limit that love by putting it into words. It is difficult, also, partly because of the sacred intimacy which it implies:

our highest and holiest thoughts often must wait for utterance because the clearest insight into the nature of God is accompanied by a diffidence that shrinks from the rudeness of words. But it is a joy, too, to speak of the love of God; for all that is tenderest in human love, — in fatherhood and motherhood, — and all that is brightest and most inspiring in human hope, is here. God is the archetype of all that is most sweet and holy in human feeling and relationship. All pure love is a ray from this central sun, a stream from this primal fountain. Hence the very perception and experience of God's love urge us to expression.

Who that has really loved has not felt this inward strife, — the restraint of love's diffidence contending with the impulse to speak.

Again, it is difficult to speak of the love of God because the message must so often meet obstruction in the minds of men. There is the cold cynicism of unbelief; there is also the criticism that springs from ignorance, littleness and grossness of nature, selfishness, and even conventional ideas of God's sovereignty, justice, and holiness. Many a professed Christian aligns himself with the unbeliever in his objection to the more ardent expressions of the divine love. How few, even in this late time, after eighteen centuries of Christianity, accept the simple, unqualified truth that "God is love"!

They say, "Yes, God loves, but—" and their

prompt and numerous limitations of the love denies their confession. Theologians have dissected the divine nature, and they have found love indeed, but only as one of many elements, and not the chief element at that. "God loves men," they tell us, "but his love cannot have its way until the wrath of his justice is appeased; and he gets wearied at last, and then love becomes spite, or awful, pitiless hate. As it is, God has favorites, — he loves Jacob, but hates Esau."

Others, less blasphemous in their representations of God, yet maintain a thought of him which makes him less lovable than a large-minded, sweet-natured man. They build walls and fences, lest the divine mercy should become vagrant, and run out where it ought not to go. It is natural, and perhaps inevitable, that human nature should limit the divine by its very modes of conceiving the divine, — should make the horizon line a boundary wall; but the horizon is only the blueness of translucent ether, that stretches on to infinity. There is no limit to the motions of the infinite Spirit. When one has in mind the conceptions of God that were current in Boehme's time, he can scarcely wonder at the great mystic's saying, "Love is greater than God!"

This great word of revelation, the greatest word of all, is the Christian preacher's chief message to all to whom it is his privilege to minister. To the young, whose earnest eyes look out on life with brave hope and chivalrous ambition, this is his message to justify their hope, to sanctify their ambition, and to give inspiration and sustenance to their spirits through whatever conflict and toil and heartache and sorrow may await them; for this alone will make life victorious at last.

To the aged and the weary this is his oft-uttered word of refreshment, as the burdens press heavier upon them and the shadows of approaching night grow longer and more chill. To those who are sick of sin and sinking down almost hopelessly in its thrall, this is his word of cheer by which they may find strength and will

"to strive, to seek, to find, and not to yield."

Many and various are the themes which he may present in the pulpit, but every sermon has one key-note, one dominant chord, and one source of inspiration; and that is always *the love of God for men*. The theme is too large for the half-hour that I may take now. The most I can do is to announce it afresh with some suggestion of its persistent and vital relation to our life and thought.

In the love of God we must find the formative and regulative principle of our philosophy, our theology, our ethics, and our art.

Let us consider *first*, for a few minutes, *the revelation* which is given in the words, "God is love," and "God so loved the world that he gave his only begotten Son, that whosoever believeth in him should not perish, but have eternal life;" then we shall consider, at greater length, some of the inferences which we may draw from the revelation.

That God loves the world because his nature is love, was and is a true revelation. It was a disclosure to the minds and hearts of men of a truth at which they had not arrived by any process of reasoning or reflection.

1. The statement was new, and the conception was new, —

"the novel thought of God that lights the world."

I do not know its parallel in ancient literature. Men believed in powerful gods, capricious gods, vindictive gods; and in some cases, as among the Hebrews, in a moral and just, and, to his own people, even merciful God; but here is a new thought: God loves the world; he is interested in his creatures, and resolved on their perfect salvation.

2. But the conception was as startling in its breadth as it was in its novelty. *God is love;* that is his nature. The extent of the divine love is measured, not by man's desert, nor even by his need, but by the infinitude of the divine nature. And this love is for *the world,* — not for a favored nation, or tribe, or family, or sect, but for humanity. Nothing must be suffered to turn our minds away from this fundamental truth. We may easily be misled by certain features of human experience.

We must interpret history by the revelation of God's love, not interpret his love by the facts of history. Our knowledge is limited, and our vision is yet dim and confused. God's love for the world gives us an interpretative principle. We may be misled by the providential election of certain individuals and nations for specific service, and conclude that for them there is something special and exclusive in the divine regard. The Hebrew had a genius for religion, the Roman for administration, and the Greek for beauty and form. The first was chosen to serve the world through the sentiment of worship and the perception of righteousness, the second through the apprehension and elaboration of law, and the third through the development of the intellect and the æsthetic sense. But these all were instrumental in the fulfilment of the divine purpose on behalf of humanity. Back of all the special vocations and particular ministries of these great peoples was the love of God, in which there is no respect of persons. The strong and the weak alike, the wise and the unwise, the just and the unjust, were the objects of the divine mercy.

In the absolute catholicity of his sympathy with men, Jesus was revelatory of the divine love. He was revelatory also of the inexhaustibleness of that love. The cross is the supreme earthly symbol of the love that can be neither conquered nor diverted from its good intention.

> "There's a wideness in God's mercy
> Like the wideness of the sea;
> There's a kindness in his justice
> That is more than liberty.
>
> "For the love of God is broader
> Than the measure of man's mind,
> And the heart of the Eternal
> Is most wonderfully kind."

And now, before I pass to a consideration of some of the inferences to be drawn from the fundamental truth which thus far we have been contemplating, let me meet some questions that may arise in your minds.

In the first place, am I not ignoring other elements in the divine nature which are essential to a true idea of God, and which condition the love of God? For example, it is commonly said that God's love is conditioned by his holiness, or the divine self-regard; by his justice, or the divine regard for law; and by his wisdom, or the divine regard for reason in dealing with dependent, weak, and sinful creatures. But all these attributes are manifestations or activities of the divine nature, which nature is perfect love. Love underlies and qualifies these, and the perfection of love insures the perfection of these. Because God is love, he will absolutely preserve his pure self-regard, will absolutely execute justice, and will absolutely exhibit and vindicate his wisdom. These are related to love as manifestation is related to nature, as action is related to law, and as method is related to purpose.

In the second place, am I not belittling the work of Christ, even rendering it superfluous? But the work of Christ is not the cause of the divine love, nor is it a device whereby love may accomplish its desire without breaking the integrity of the divine law. It is, on the contrary, a revelation of God with power, and a demonstration of the truth that "where sin abounded, grace did much more abound." Christ giving himself in utter self-sacrifice for humanity is not a substitute for the fulfilment of the divine law in human nature, but a means to that fulfilment. The whole process of human redemption is a revelation and result of the love which is absolute and eternal. This is true, if we hold with St. Paul that in Christ " dwelt all the fulness of the Godhead bodily;" it would be true if Christ were only perfect man, for the entire significance of his life and death lies in the revelation of God which was made in and through him. There is a perfect correspondence between the words of Jesus, "I came not to do mine own will, but the will of him who sent me," and St. Paul's words, "God was in Christ reconciling the world unto himself."

What are some of the more important inferences which we may legitimately draw from this fundamental truth, that the nature of God is perfect love, and that the will of God is the purpose of perfect love?

1. We find in this truth the reason and motive for creation. Our philosophy of the world must base itself on the love of God, in order to be stable and satisfying. Because God is love, he creates, — objectifying his thought in countless forms of being, and at once expressing and satisfying his own nature in the evolution of the cosmos. Once we were accustomed to think of creation as a divine act accomplished in the remote past; but with wider knowledge of the world we have come to see that creation is not a single act, but a process that, beginning in the infinite past, is still going on. The ends of that process are not material, but moral. The physical universe is but the arena of the spiritual universe which is unfolding under the impulse of the Infinite Poet, — ποιήτης, — or Maker. What we call redemption is but the fashioning of this spiritual universe.

So for love God made the worlds, wove the glorious garment of star-sown sky, and prepared, through long ages of change, the habitable globe, whereon

". . . at last arose the man

"Who throve and branched from clime to clime,
   The herald of a higher race,
   And of himself in higher place,
If so he types this work of time

"Within himself, from more to more;
   Or crowned with attributes of woe
   Like glories, move his course, and show
That life is not an idle ore,

> "But iron dug from central gloom,
> And heated hot with burning fears,
> And dipt in baths of hissing tears,
> And battered with the shocks of doom
>
> "To shape and use."

There is a truth in the teachings of the old theologians that God made the world for his own glory; yet often this idea was so conceived and so put as to come perilously near a representation on a large scale of Nebuchadnezzar strutting about the royal palace in his capital city and boasting: "Is not this great Babylon which I have built for the royal dwelling-place, by the might of my power and for the glory of my majesty?" Rightly and reverently apprehending the divine purpose in creation, we may truly say that God created all things for his own glory; and, as his glory is the manifestation of his own perfect nature, his love supplies at once the motive and the end of the creation, which, as far as it lies within our ken, he is bringing to completion in the salvation of the world.

2. A second inference which we are bound to draw is: If God loves the world, it is not a hopelessly bad world; it is not a scene of defeat and wreck, — a fair beginning marred and ruined by a diabolical intelligence, — but a field of germs and promise, a sphere and opportunity for divine love's great achievement. An Oriental myth, apparently having no place in Hebrew literature

before the exile, and to which neither the prophets nor Jesus ever allude, in the hands of theologians and commentators and the great Puritan poet, Milton, has fixed in the general Christian mind an idea of the world which makes it the peculiar domain of Satan. But the love which created the world possesses and rules it. It is not the devil's world, but God's world; and he is in it, bringing out the permanent good against the dark foil of the transient evil, promoting every right endeavor, conserving every right achievement, and suffering no pure purpose and aspiration to fail of their final aim.

I know that many devoted Christians look upon the enterprise of God in Christ as mainly, if not entirely, an enterprise of rescue and repair; but I am persuaded that a deeper knowledge of God, and a clearer insight into his purpose, which a radical view of the divine nature as love must impart, will change their conception of the world, and will give them new heart and hope as they grapple with the problems of present evil and sorrow and wrong. We toil not in an alien land; we fight not in an enemy's country. The old hymn says truly,

"We're marching through Immanuel's ground;"

it may be, as the hymn continues,

"To fairer worlds on high;"

but this world, sacred with holy memories, consecrated by the footprints and by the cross of the Son of God, and rich with beauties of aspect and the meanings of human experience that forever incite poet and artist to their highest achievements, is fair enough and great enough for the consummate flowering and fulfilment of a redeemed and heavenly life.

Whatever other worlds there may be, we know that here God may and does tabernacle with men, and here he may yet show glories of which prophet and seer have not dreamed.

3. Another inference, closely joined with both the preceding, is: If God loves the world, he surely administers it for good, — not relatively, nor conditionally, but absolutely. I know I tread on ground here that is considered dangerous; but I walk fearlessly. With the Church of all the centuries I confess: "I believe in God the Father Almighty;" and against the narrow hope which, in their doubt and weakness, so large a number of her children have cherished, I proclaim the larger hope which she has never wholly lost since Jesus said: "And I, if I be lifted up from the earth, will draw all men unto myself." Against the pessimism of much of the theology and the common thought of Christians, I bear the testimony of that faith which bases itself immovably on the universal and unconquerable love of God, "who is the Saviour of all men, especially of them that believe." It is not faith, but fear, that holds us

back from grasping the greatness of God's purpose and the certainty of his ultimate end in creation.

The law of the world is progress along the line of a spiritual evolution. The life of the world is better to-day than it ever has been in the past. The love of God is our surety that it will grow better and better under the divine tuition and discipline, until even the Son of God "shall see of the travail of his soul and be satisfied." But are there not pain and penalty and sin and death? Yes, but in and over these is the unconquerable love of God. But if God is invincible love, how can he punish? How can he maintain and vindicate his righteous law? Because he loves he will wield the lash of retributive penalty and kindle Gehenna fires to feed upon the impurities of human life. Pain is an instrument, not a finality. But this is love's triumph, that it will be known and welcomed at last. Because God loves the world, the kingdoms of the world will become the kingdom of our Lord and of his Christ.

The faith which the love of God inspires, does not make light of sin; it does not shut the eyes to the dark problem of evil; it does not empty the future of terrors for the wilful sinner; but it does stand fast in the trembling and awful, yet happy confidence, that God is supreme, and that divine love will have its way at last, and "every knee shall bow, and every tongue shall confess with thanksgiving that Jesus Christ is Lord, to the glory of God the Father."

Day by day this larger hope, springing out of a deepening faith, is growing in the heart of the Church. Day by day the number increases of those who

> "grow too great
> For narrow creeds of right and wrong, which fade
> Before the unmeasured thirst for good: while peace
> Rises within them ever more and more.
> Such men are even now upon the earth,
> Serene amid the half-formed creatures round
> Who should be saved by them and joined with them."

4. A final inference bears directly on the motive of the individual life. If God loves the world, then surely we should love it, and pour our lives into the endeavor for its salvation. God's motive must be our motive; love and love's labor must fill our hearts and hands. Here is the law of our life. So I beseech you, my friends, open your hearts to the great and precious truth of God's Word. God is love, and love is law. Let the perfect love of God fill you with invincible hope. In the struggle with sin, in the trial of pain and sorrow, in the bitterness of disappointment, in the anguish of life's seeming defeat, hold fast to the truth that God loves you, that he loves the world, and that he is saving the world and you, and bringing you surely, if to you it seem slowly, to the fulfilment of life and the perfect realisation of his blessed will. Do not fear to

trust him utterly; do not fail to obey him loyally; and then, whatever may befall you here, you can say, with Whittier, —

> "I know not where His islands lift
> Their fronded palms in air;
> I only know I cannot drift
> Beyond his love and care."

III.

THE KINGDOM OF GOD.

I would not fix the time, the day, nor hour,
   When thou with all thine angels shalt appear;
When in thy kingdom thou shalt come with power;
   E'en now, perhaps, the promised day is near!

For though in slumber deep the world may lie,
   And e'en thy Church forget thy great command,
Still, year by year thy coming draweth nigh!
   And in its power thy kingdom is at hand.

Not in some future world alone 't will be,
   Beyond the grave, beyond the bounds of time;
But on the earth thy glory we shall see,
   And share thy triumph, peaceful, pure, sublime.

JONES VERY.

III.

THE KINGDOM OF GOD.

Thy kingdom come. Thy will be done, as in heaven, so on earth. — MATT. vi. 10.

NO saying of Christ's is more impressive, or more comprehensive in its implication of divine purpose, than that one immediately following the words: "Do ye, therefore, pray after this manner." The Lord's Prayer, as by universal consent it is called, is the prayer of the whole Christian Church.

Without doing the language of Christ any violence, we may say that in this brief utterance are expressed or implied all the essential elements of a spiritual faith, the essential principles of a spiritual life, and the essential pledge of a spiritual destiny. If there are doctrines, or precepts, that have been inculcated as Christian, which are inconsistent with this prayer, or have no unforced implication in this prayer, we may well question whether those doctrines or precepts belong to the fundamental faith, or ethics, of Christianity. Certainly the entire teaching of Jesus, as reported by the Evangelists, is here, expressly or by implication. The progress of eighteen hundred years suggests to the thoughtful mind no necessity of revising this simple yet all-inclusive petition. It stands to-day as the succinct and comprehensive expression of the purest longing, the largest aspiration, and the loftiest ideal of humanity in its relation to God. It belongs to no sect, no nation, and no period of time, but to all the world and to all time. It is the perpetual witness to the divine origin and spiritual destiny of man, as well as to the Being, Sovereignty, and Fatherhood of God. In the proportion that men make this prayer their own, they enter into and consciously appropriate the divine purpose which, through the long procession of the ages, is accomplishing, —

> "The one far-off divine event
> To which the whole creation moves."

The clause which we are now to study is itself a petition so broad in its scope that, at times, all other forms of prayer seem superfluous. "Thy kingdom come,"— it is the cry that Divine Fatherhood may become manifest Sovereignty. "Thy will be done, as in heaven, so on earth,"— it is the soul's confession of utter submission and homage and faith towards the Sovereign Fatherhood that rules the universe, and attains the ends for which the universe exists. This petition is the whole of prayer put into one strong, comprehensive sentence; and this sentence is the heart of the Lord's

Prayer. What precedes it is pure expression of worship. What follows it is simple specialization of life's daily needs and daily duty. Everything that we can wish, or hope, or think of good is involved in the fulfilment of this all-embracing aspiration, " Thy kingdom come."

1. In the first place, these words express much more than simple petition; there is in them *a confession that the world is not what it might be.* The kingdom of God, as the perfect embodiment and expression of divine order and beauty and beneficence, is not clearly manifest now. The world is the scene of much disorder. Men are ignorant, bestial, and selfish, in almost all conceivable degrees of ignorance, bestiality, and selfishness. Love between man and man is far from being dominant. Sin and sorrow alike widely prevail. The history of human life is a history of progress; but it is also a history of struggle and tempest and dark tragedy. Justice is not infallibly done; for often the wicked prosper, and the good are oppressed. The evils of life are vast and manifold. Poverty and wretchedness hold great multitudes in a bitter and hopeless bondage. Grief and pain, sooner or later, visit every heart. The best men fail not only of their ideal, but even of that which confessedly they might attain.

Every human life is an illustration of incompleteness. Every conscience testifies of sin. Every soul is an embodied want. Society — the complex organism in which individuals are held in a common life and vitally joined in the fulfilment of a common destiny — is the defective, disorganized, and suffering individual "writ large."

Humanity, one in origin, one in essential nature, and one in the great obligations of the moral life, is yet a congeries of diverse and more or less conflicting races and nationalities. Some of these races are far advanced in civilization; others still linger on the dark borders of barbarism; and others still abide in a condition scarcely raised above that of the brutes. As, even in the nations farthest advanced in intelligence and virtue, the law of love is still imperfectly fulfilled, and individual strives with individual and class strives with class in selfish competition, so between the various nations and tribes of men there is perpetual jealousy and mistrust, and threat of conflict. At this moment the great powers of Europe, armed to the teeth, maintain a precarious peace.

That the general moral condition of the world is better now than it ever has been in the past, will be admitted, I think, by the most cautious critic. But, putting the best possible construction on all that we learn of the life of humankind, we must confess that the world is still very far from that condition of intelligence, virtue, harmony and goodwill, which is involved in the least imaginative and least aspiring conception of the kingdom of God.

The Christian heart, in the very cry, " Thy kingdom come," confesses, not the ruin of the world, not the failure, the defeat, but the incomplete, the still waiting fulfilment, of God's will in the world. The superficial optimist who declares that all that is is the best, and obstinately shuts his eyes to the evil and want and wretchedness and sin which everywhere appear in human life, is unable to apprehend the deep meaning of the Christian prayer.

Let the truth be faced bravely. The world is not what it should be, nor what it might be. There is evil, hideous and vast. "The whole creation groaneth and travaileth in pain," waiting for a deliverance which has not yet come. The soul does face the truth in uttering this prayer, "Thy kingdom come."

2. But the acknowledgment of incompleteness, disorder and sin in the world, is accompanied by an expression of *trust in the divine righteousness and good purpose*. This trust is not broken down by the ever-present spectacle — which to the finite eye is so appalling — of defect in the present condition and apparent tendency of human life. The perception of the divine excellence, which the devout mind increasingly attains, sharpens rather than lessens the contrast between that which is and that which ought to be. The more one knows of God, the more clearly he sees the imperfections both of the individual man and of human society. But the increasing revelation of defect in human life, mediated by increasing perception of

the divine ideal, begets neither despair nor resentment. The belief in God, which this prayer expresses, saves us from pessimism. As an unflinching recognition of the facts of life destroys the superficial optimism which says that all that is is the best, so a living faith in God destroys the equally superficial pessimism which says that whatever is is worst. Faith in God involves such a sense of the divine goodness and righteousness as assures the heart of the ultimate triumph of good throughout the whole empire of God. The cry of passionate desire, " Thy kingdom come," is immediately followed by the word of patient and hopeful resignation, " Thy will be done, as in heaven, so on earth." This resignation is not a passive and unaspiring content with life and the world as they are, but it is a faithful acceptance of God's sovereignty, and God's purpose, and God's method. It is an expectant and trustful submission to the supreme will, which is felt to be both absolutely good, and, in its own time, absolutely efficient.

> " Fierce though the fiends may fight,
> And long though the angels hide,
> I know that truth and right
> Have the universe on their side."

The spirit of loyal obedience to God is joined with uncomplaining endurance of what seems the hardness of his will and the slowness of his action.

The imperfection and disorder of the world

touch all of us. Each of us has to endure, not only his own individual weakness and sinfulness and disappointment and pain, but each of us has to bear also the strain and shock of the multiform wrong that works in society about us. We are involved in a common lot. We suffer innumerable ills that are not the result of our individual imperfection or fault. Other men's sins scourge us; other men's ignorance hinders and burdens us; other men's woes aggravate our sorrow. There seems, sometimes, a hideous wrong in that solidarity of society by which the innocent are made to suffer with the guilty; but that very solidarity is the necessary condition of the worldwide salvation which God is accomplishing. By it we are made participant in vast benefits that are not the result of our individual effort or merit. Other men's virtues enrich and strengthen us; other men's knowledge and insight make our path clearer and our load lighter; other men's joys mitigate our sorrows; and other men's pangs expiate our guilt. There is a vast beneficent side to this relation in which we are bound to the totality of human life.

Moreover, often wrong appears to be triumphant because of the limitation of our view. We must walk by faith and not by sight, because, as yet, our sight is dim. In a true sense, indeed, faith in God is sight. If we really believe in God, and in that belief say, "Thy kingdom come, thy will be done on earth as it is in heaven," then, in so far as we make this prayer truly, we rise to God's horizon, and we see things from his point of view. Recognizing the evil in the world, and in our own lives, we yet affirm that the evil of the world is transient; that what appears evil is often only " good in the making; " that behind the apparent disorder is a growing order; that goodness is at the heart of the universe; that "righteousness and judgment are the habitation of God's throne; " and that not the present state, considered by itself, is best, but that God's will is best, and that God's will is getting itself done in sure, if seemingly slow, ways.

Such affirmation of faith the heart makes that, without passive content, is patient, that without despair is resigned, that, while holding fast to the ideal, yet cheerfully and trustfully accepts the real, and amid its forbidding facts maintains the happy assurance of the good that is and is to be.

3. But still more than it expresses acknowledgment of the evil that is, and resignation to the will of God in our present lot, does this prayer express *an aspiration and an ideal.* The largeness of true Christianity is in this prayer. Jesus always contemplates humanity, as well as the individual. Of all the apostles, St. Paul most closely follows him in this. As the salvation of the individual soul is not a mere rescue from penalty, but a process of spiritual quickening and unfolding toward "the perfect man," so the salvation of the world is not

a meagrely successful struggle with a great catastrophe, — a life-boat expedition among the helpless and sinking victims of a wreck, — but the spiritual quickening of humanity and its unfolding toward the perfect society, which is the realized and manifest kingdom of God.

The process of the salvation of the world is a process of divine inspiration, and discipline, and development. Supernatural in its origin, both because of the supernatural source from which it springs and the supernatural personalities with which it deals, the salvation of humanity is supernatural in its whole course. It is supernatural, not in the sense of mere miracle or of arbitrary disregard of natural law, but in the only true and large sense, that it is a spiritual process of which the natural order is the basis. The Christian ideal is the rule of the spirit over the flesh; the fulfilment and coronation of nature with the supernature; the complete emergence of man from ignorance and sin and weakness into wisdom and holiness and power; the perfection of the individual in and through the perfection of society; and the perfect manifestation of the Creative and Immanent Life in the nature, relations, and activities of the creature, — that is, the glorious revelation of God in a spiritual cosmos, in which are gathered up all the results of man's entire history, and which, in its order and beauty and blessedness, fulfils the prophetic intimations of divine teaching and human experience. In a word, the Christian ideal is the kingdom of God; and the kingdom of God is not a new creation, save as the flowering and fruitage of the divine purpose in the old are new. It is not a state superimposed on the world from above, but the world redeemed, purified, disciplined, and spiritualized, and so carried up to a higher plane. There is no break in the continuity of God's working.

The Christian aspiration for the coming of the kingdom of God is, then, an aspiration for the advancement and completion of a process now going on. That process is far more positive than it is negative. It includes the judgment and destruction of evil, but still more the affirmation and fulfilment of the good. The kingdom of God as the perfect ideal covers the whole field of life. It means the salvation of the individual man by the disclosure of his individual relations to God, his individual guilt and need, and his individual capacities for truth and righteousness, and by the regeneration of the individual spirit, that this disclosure may have at once its justification and its true issue in individual peace and joy, and growth in all the graces and powers of the spiritual life.

But the spiritual life is not exclusive of the natural life. That is, the man is not removed, by the awakening of his spirit, from the conflicts and duties and discipline of daily experience. In so far as the kingdom of God is the salvation of the individual, it is the consecration and elevation of the whole life of the individual. It involves all of the needs, obligations, activities, aspirations, and possibilities that pertain to man from the beginning of his existence. It exhibits the real significance of all his material and intellectual relations and experiences. It co-ordinates with the high aims of the awakened spirit, the daily business, the domestic ties, the political functions, — all, indeed, that belongs to the natural and proper life of man in the world. The kingdom of God, therefore, in so far as it has realization in the individual man, means better life, higher aspiration, greater skill as a worker, greater range and power as a thinker, richer culture of mind and person, a tenderer grace in the home, a finer morality in trade, a nobler ambition in society, a more scrupulous unselfishness and a larger comprehension both of rights and duties in politics, a wider horizon in views of life, a broader sympathy with mankind, a quickened sense of kinship with his fellows, a more capacious charity, and a solider strength of character. It means, in a word, the consecration, enlargement, and many-sided improvement of the individual man, here and now. There is no arbitrary postponement of perfection to a future state, but a daily growth and endeavor toward the perfection in the attainment of which the future is inseparably linked with all the past, and thus the divine education of the human soul is fulfilled.

But the kingdom of God means also the salvation of society in its organic life. God is related to men, but he is related also to mankind. The corporate life of humanity is not less real than the life of the single personality. The salvation of society is the salvation of the individual extended throughout the sphere of his manifold relations. It includes, then, the regeneration of the social personality, the quickening and enlargement of the social intelligence, the purification and refinement of the social character, the development of all the social activities, and the realization in social forms of the spiritual graces of love, truth, and righteousness.

The separation which many make between the redemption of the individual and the redemption of society is fatal to any true conception, as it would be fatal, were it actual, to any true realization, of the kingdom of God. By that separation the industries and arts and politics of men are left out of the spiritual realm. A powerful disorganizing force is thus set in motion in society. Men attempt to live a Christian life in the church and a secular life in the world. They are overpowered by the world because of the very weakness which their misconception breeds. There is no sacredness attaching to the church, which ought not also to attach to the chamber of commerce. There is no honor that marks the bond of brother with brother in "the communion of saints," which ought not also to mark the bond of employer with employed, of seller with buyer, and of producer with consumer. There is no ground in Christian thought for the sort of distinction which perpetually is made between the sacred and the secular. The kingdom of God is all-inclusive. It gathers up in its significance the whole of life. It means better laws, better social customs, better industrial relations, better economic principles, better public works, better amusements, better sanitary conditions, better streets and conveyances and houses, better municipal administration, better art, better schools, better newspapers, better books, better everything. Its claims are absolutely inclusive, and its consecration spreads, like subtle perfume, everywhere.

In this large conception of the kingdom of God the individual Christian life receives a great enlargement. The aspiration of the individual soul for a fuller experience of divine grace becomes an aspiration for the suffusion of society with the quickening tides of the Spirit. The longing of the individual soul for holiness becomes a longing for the spiritual health of humanity. The selfishness that so readily and so often creeps into the religious life to contract and corrupt it is shut out. The individual lives in the widened consciousness of his wide relationship. Love becomes operative in the most secret motions of his spirit. His sympathies reach out for the world, and his thinking broadens to the breadth of his sympathy. His life is deepened and enlarged on every side. The social significance of Christianity, possessing his mind, makes his whole nature susceptible to the social forces of Christianity. He escapes isolation. He is emancipated from the bonds, not of conviction, but of sectarianism and partisanship; and the ties that bind him to his fellows become attractions constraining him to all beneficent and philanthropic endeavor.

The individual soul, under the Christian idea, types the society, the nation, the race. The supreme law of the individual life is love: "Thou shalt love the Lord thy God with all thy heart, and with all thy soul, and with all thy mind, and with all thy strength, . . . and . . . thou shalt love thy neighbor as thyself. On these two commandments hang all the law and the prophets." Love is thus the ground of ethics, the spring of motive, and the regnant principle of all action. It is the law and the pervading spirit of the kingdom of God. It is thus the deep-lying bond of social unity. The aspiration for the coming of the kingdom of God is an aspiration for the universal rule of love, and the diffusion throughout the world of those benefits of comfort, peace, knowledge, liberty, righteousness and joy, which love brings in its bosom. This means that unselfish love shall be the motive in labor, in trade, in invention, in teaching, in governing, in everything.

Here is the ideal, so beautiful, and, in the face of actual human life, seemingly so unreal. But the unattained is ever the unreal to the dull mind and sordid spirit. The soul that believes in God believes in the fulfilment of God's purpose, that is, in the realization of the kingdom of God. The day may seem far off, but it is coming. The universal reign of love, creating new economics, a new commerce, new politics, a new social life, supplanting greed of gain with passion for service, and mutual competition with mutual helpfulness, unreal as it seems to us, immersed in the struggle and held by the habits and ruled by the ideas of to-day, is yet the destined result and fulfilment of the centuries and ages of divine teaching and discipline. The brooding life of God in the world will beget all the glory and blessedness of which the rapt seer has caught the symbol in the New Jerusalem, — the city that lieth four-square, — the type of perfected social organization. Every time this prayer is sincerely uttered, there is affirmation of the faith that grasps the coming realization of God's purpose, and of the pledge which is made by the Son of God in giving this prayer and giving himself on the cross of utter self-sacrifice for the salvation of the world.

4. Thus, finally, this prayer expresses *a supreme hope and a supreme endeavor*. The grand end of life, from the Christian point of view, is the kingdom of God. In this hope are gathered up all

high and sweet hopes that blossom in the heart of the man of good-will and in the heart of society. In this endeavor are included all right endeavors of individuals and communities. Materially, every invention that gives man a larger and easier mastery over nature, and liberates his spirit a little more from the necessity of continual drudging, promotes the coming of the kingdom. Intellectually, every contribution to man's knowledge of the earth, the history of the race, and the nature and possibilities of his own soul, and every diffusion of knowledge through a wider circle of men, promotes the coming of the kingdom. Morally and spiritually, every deed done, every thought uttered, every sacrifice made for the emancipation of men from ignorance, sin, vice, and wretchedness, and every new infusion of faith, hope, and love into human hearts, promotes the coming of the kingdom. All right endeavors are coordinated and carried forward to their true end by this conception of the kingdom. The pulse of the divine love, expressing itself in enterprises of philanthropy and Christian missions, beats in this hope. The force of the divine purpose, recreating the social order of men in righteousness, works in this endeavor.

Under the rule of this idea of the kingdom of God, the co-working of man with God becomes a practical, daily experience. Religious activity loses in peculiarity, and gains in sincerity and breadth and power. The church discovers its true and universal function. Its mission relates it to the whole of life, and not merely to individual men and women; and so its function is not merely that of an isolated witness of divine truth, — a Pharos flashing its light across a dark and tempestuous sea, — but that of an embodied love and life, bearing the sweet contagion of universal health into all the members of the great race-body which is meant to be the body of Christ.

How much it means, then, to utter this prayer, "Thy kingdom come. Thy will be done, as in heaven, so on earth." It means that we are committed to that faith, that aspiration, that hope and that endeavor which have their end and fulfilment in the redemption of the world. It means that we are set to the task of living the individual life of trust and obedience and love. It means that we are seeking knowledge and power and grace for the service of our fellowmen. It means that we are practising in all our business and pleasure the principles of the gospel of Christ. It means that we are helping those about us to a true knowledge of God and a life in the spirit. It means that we are consecrating the commonest industries with a loving temper. It means that we are resisting the sharp competitions and corroding jealousies and destructive selfishness which still so widely and hurtfully pervade the life of men. It means that we are living in the thought of our relations to humanity, and in our aspirations, our longings, our sufferings, and our prayers, are carrying with us the need and sorrow and sin of the whole world. It means, in a word, that by word and deed, by desire and purpose, we are seeking in ourselves, in our homes, in society, and in the world, the fulfilment of our prayer, — the ever more perfect reign of love, and thus the realization of the kingdom of God.

> " Say not, the struggle naught availeth,
>   The labor and the wounds are vain,
> The enemy faints not nor faileth,
>   And as things have been they remain.
>
> " If hopes were dupes, fears may be liars.
>   It may be, in yon smoke concealed,
> Your comrades chase e'en now the flyers,
>   And but for you possess the field.
>
> " For while the tired waves, vainly breaking,
>   Seem here no painful inch to gain,
> Far back, through creeks and inlets making,
>   Comes silent, flooding in, the main.
>
> " And not by eastern windows only
>   When morning comes, comes in the light;
> In front the sun climbs slow, how slowly,
>   But, westward, look ! the land is bright."

IV.

THE COMING OF CHRIST.

I SING the Birth was born to-night,
The Author both of life and light;
　　The angels so did sound it: —
And like the ravished shepherds said,
Who saw the light, and were afraid,
　　Yet searched, and true they found it.

The Son of God, the eternal King,
That did us all salvation bring,
　　And freed the soul from danger;
He whom the whole world could not take,
The Word, which heaven and earth did make,
　　Was now laid in a manger.

What comfort by him do we win,
Who made himself the price of sin,
　　To make us heirs of glory!
To see this Babe, all innocence,
A martyr born in our defence! —
　　Can man forget this story?

　　　　　　　　　　　BEN JONSON.

IV.

THE COMING OF CHRIST.[1]

Faithful is the saying, and worthy of all acceptation, that Christ Jesus came into the world to save sinners. — 1 TIM. i. 15.

THIS is part of an autobiographical note, for St. Paul goes on to say: "of whom I am chief: howbeit for this cause I obtained mercy, that in me as chief might Jesus Christ show forth all his long-suffering;" yet it states a primary fact and a fundamental truth of Christianity. The fact is the coming of Jesus; the truth is that Jesus came to save the world from sin. I ask you to consider this truth with me now, because of its appropriateness to the season, and because it represents so large and vital a part of Christian teaching and preaching.

The Christmas festivities are at hand; we celebrate the birth of Jesus Christ. Whatever may be our private reasons for observing the Christmas festival, the true deep reason and motive lie in this fact, that nearly nineteen hundred years ago there was born of a lowly Jewish mother, in a little town in Palestine, a baby who was known as the child of

[1] A Christmas sermon.

Joseph and Mary, and whose name was called Jesus, which means "Saviour." Is it not an extraordinary thing? Nations instinctively celebrate the birthdays of their own heroes and benefactors; but all nations of Christendom celebrate the birthday of a Jew! The history of the past eighteen centuries is indissolubly associated with the name of Jesus. No other name is so woven into its very texture. A few years ago, in Paris, one might see everywhere, carved on the stone walls of public buildings, wrought into fabrics, and graven on monuments, the letter N. It was the mark and sign of the emperor. The name of Jesus is indelibly stamped on the civilization and inextricably woven into the literature of the world.

It is because, in some way, the weal of humanity is inseparably joined with the name, the life, the teachings, the deeds, and the personality of Jesus; it is because in Jesus, as in no one else, the world finds a revelation of God and a "promise and potency" of salvation; it is because, in a word, men discover in Jesus, not a Jew, nor an Oriental, nor a mere genius, nor a philanthropist, nor a martyr, but a Son of Man, who is also the Son of God, in whom the spiritual world visibly and palpably discloses itself for the enlightenment, comfort, and emancipation of mankind, — that the birthday of Jesus has become the great, gladsome festival of all Christendom.

It is a truism, perhaps, but one that must be

uttered again and again, that man's deepest needs are spiritual. More urgent than the hunger for bread, deeper than the need of industrial and political liberty, when once men awaken, is their hunger for that which feeds the heart, and their need of the liberty of the spirit. Love and truth and righteousness have a value greater than any material possessions; and until these are found, an incurable unrest cankers the human soul.

Jesus Christ meets the deepest needs, he brings an answer even to the unexpressed wants, of the human spirit. In him the soul's cry for God, its longing for peace, and its capacity for hope, find a response and supply not found in any one else.

But it is not possible, save by a violent dislocation, to separate the spiritual from the intellectual and the material. All these are interwoven. Men have tried to separate them; especially have they tried to separate the religious from the secular, and the life of the spirit from the life of the senses and passions. In so far as they have been successful in this effort they have marred the integrity and hindered the completion of life. Robert Browning, the poet of life in its totality, wrote, —

> "Not soul helps flesh more now
> Than flesh helps soul."

"Flesh," that is the totality of the life of the senses, and "soul," that is the totality of the life of the spirit, belong in a single unity of personal being. In the true life, pleasure, study, industry, and worship are co-operant. There is nothing incongruous between the various powers and activities of the normal man.

But Browning's word applies also to society, — the individual man writ large. The essential wants of any one man are the essential wants of humanity. Form and manifestation are multifold; but the race is wholly one in its fundamental affinities and needs. Truth, righteousness, love — in one word, God, is the answer to the deepest human aspiration and desire and need.

Jesus is related to all the various phases of human life. He is in touch with childhood and age, with manhood and womanhood, with the rich and the poor, with the ignorant and the wise, with the good and the bad, — that is, he is in touch with their humanity. At every point of actual human nature he is in sympathetic contact.

Other great men are insular; Jesus is universal. If he seem insular to us, it is because we do not know him; he has been misrepresented, and men have sought to shut up the gracious wealth of his personality within the narrow lines of dogma. His relation to human life is one of entire understanding and sympathy, and of beneficent power and intention. His purpose toward mankind is a purpose of salvation in its full scope.

Before he was born it was said of him, "His name shall be called Jesus, for he shall save his people from their sins." His people is humanity, for he claimed and claims the world. Looking back over the centuries since Jesus was a baby in Bethlehem, we see that his unvarying real relation to men is that of Saviour. The Evangelist's word is the statement of prophecy and expectation; St. Paul's word is the statement of experience. Out of his own experience the apostle testified: "Faithful is the saying, and worthy of all acceptation, that Christ Jesus came into the world to save sinners." This is the continuous testimony of experience, — the experience of all who have really known Jesus. Men have speculated about him, debated about him, desiccated his teachings into dogmas, and turned his words of love into shibboleths; but they have not known him until they have known him as a Saviour from sin and unrest and despair. He brought to the world no scheme of salvation full of conditions and equipped with a vast machinery of ordinances and sacrifices and ritual. He simply testified of God, and exhibited truth in a character of perfect sweetness and symmetry and strength, and lived in utter and unconstrained subjection to the law of love. His life was at once a sermon and a service, all the meaning and end of which were salvation.

Because Jesus thus relates himself, not to parties and churches, but to humanity as a divine-human Saviour, and in that relation is concerned with the totality of human life, we celebrate his birth. In celebrating the birth of Christ we re-announce and re-emphasize the purpose for which he came into the world. In the serious heart, beneath all the festivity and the interchange of gifts which so fitly and delightfully mark the Christmas season, is this truth, — Jesus Christ came into the world to save sinners, and to save them from their sins. If we can only take in the full scope of this truth, we shall find the solution of life's darkest problems and the spring of inexhaustible hope and joy.

That word " sin " is a most interesting word. It means " missing the mark," therefore erring, wandering, going wrong. It is a very comprehensive word, and there is in it a suggestion of large tenderness. To sin is to miss the mark, to go astray from the true aim of life. To fail of doing the right and of attaining the good is included, as well as doing evil.

Sin is always a blunder. How much of sin we can see to be just that. The ignorance, the animalism, the blindness, and the selfishness of men lie at the root and are the source of specific acts of sinfulness. These are only symptomatic of condition; and that condition is not one of inherent malicious depravity. The " total depravity " that figures so largely in the Calvinistic theology, if it exist at all, is not a primary, nor even a secondary condition of human nature; it is an advanced stage of development in the wrong direction. The most suggestive examples of depravity in the New

Testament are not found among the "publicans and harlots," but among the " Pharisees." On the whole, the New Testament, at least the Gospels, deal gently with sin. This is true particularly of Jesus. How patient he is with human nature! illustrating the Psalmist's saying : " Like as a father pitieth his children, so the Lord pitieth them that fear him ; for he knoweth our frame, he remembereth that we are dust!"

The one form of sin which Jesus smites as with a thunderbolt is the self-righteousness that reveals itself in pride, in censoriousness, in hardness and pitilessness of heart, and in self-induced spiritual blindness, joined with the pretence of eminent sanctity and claims of infallible religious authority. This is what the law calls *laesa majestas ;* Pharisaism is a violation of the majesty of divine love. The Pharisees alone Jesus denounced. There seems to be no other way to deal with the Pharisee than to shatter him with a lightning stroke of indignation and judgment. To the publican and harlot, the victim of passions and vices and ignorance, how gentle and patient he was! The incident of the woman "that was a sinner," at the house of Simon the Pharisee, and the parable of the prodigal son, are representative and revelatory of Christ's attitude toward sinners ; and we are warranted by Christ's teaching in believing that these are representative and revelatory of God's attitude toward sinners.

How true it is that all sinning is a missing the mark! It is turning aside into the wrong way; it is missing or defeating one's true purpose in the world; it is failing to attain the real good of life. Does not the sinner of every sort miss the mark? There is no value in any end that is separated from integrity and purity and faith and unselfishness. The term " sin " is inclusive of the thousand wrong deeds that we do; but, more than that, it characterizes our generic course in evil. It includes disposition as well as act; condition as well as conduct; and the omission of the good we might do and attain as well as the commission of positive evil.

Now Jesus came into the world, came forth from God, to save sinners, — not primarily from penalty, but from their sins; to turn those who, in ignorance or selfishness, were missing the mark, into the right way; to quicken them with the life and enrich them with the wisdom of God; to beget them anew in spiritual disposition. " To as many as received him he gave the right to become children of God ": that is, the prodigal, restored, becomes, in spirit as well as in name, the son; the " lost " is " found," and he that was " dead " lives again. In a word, Jesus came to save men from sin by developing in them, through their faith and love, the righteousness of God.

We may phrase it as we please, emphasize this feature or that of the process which in the language of theology is called "the plan of salvation;" but this is the great aim and constant endeavor of Jesus: to save men from their sins by the power of the divine life in them, communicated through him who came that they might have life, and have it abundantly, and thus to make of them new men, spiritual men, in whom God's purpose should move toward its fair fulfilment, — men who should no longer miss the mark, but speed or climb toward the goal of "the perfect man, the measure of the stature of the fulness of Christ."

The philosophy of religious experience, from the Christian point of view, is thus put by St. Paul: "If any man be in Christ he is a new creature." He is not simply the old creature newly placed, carrying over across the chasm of an emotional paroxysm all his old prejudices, ignorances, enmities, uncharitablenesses, and the like; nor another creature, the result of some sudden down-rush of magical transforming power, — but a new creature, because touched with new life from God, newly adjusted within to the divine law, newly awakened to love, charged with a new purpose, and inspired with a new hope.

Men used to ask the young Christian, or the man just awakened to spiritual life: "What evidence have you that you have experienced a change of heart?" — a most unnecessary and often unreal question. Life is evidenced by its product, not by the profession, which often advertises its counterfeit. The man whom the Son of God has quickened to new life is busy living along the new lines of purpose and aspiration, too busy to indulge in morbid introspection. If the question really arises as to whether one is a Christian or not, it is answered by one's manifest affinities with Christ in serving men. The dull and ignorant servant girl perceived that she was different from what she had been because, now, she "swept under the mats." That meant a finer honesty in her daily life. The test is good. You men to whom Christ has come, how about the daily transactions in the market and the daily conduct in the home? Salvation reveals itself in a nobler purpose, a purer virtue, a gentler spirit, and a richer unselfishness in the daily living.

As "sin" is so comprehensive a word, including all error, failure, and defect, as well as all positive maleficence, including the entire imperfection of man, so, on the other hand, "salvation" is a comprehensive word, including all aspiration and purpose that reach toward a better life and character, all progression and fulfilment of the man who is now but germinal, all experience of the unfolding and perfecting life of the child of God. It is so much more than the dismissal of a convicted but pardoned culprit, so much more than an escape from deserved and imminent punishment, that as one enters into its deep meaning he forgets that this was any part of it, save as he can never forget the sweet joy of forgiveness which comes to him in that consciousness of God into which Christ brings him. Salvation becomes the achieving of a life, the fulfilment of a divine destiny.

In the accomplishment of his purpose of salvation Jesus relates himself both to the individual soul and to society. When we contemplate what he does for this or that particular man, we see but one aspect of his work. The creation of the new man is no more his work than is the creation of the new society. "The kingdom of God" is the regenerated society, as "the child of God" is the regenerated individual soul.

Society is deep in sin. It, too, misses the mark in many and grievous ways. Through the ignorance and selfishness of men and classes of men, it fails to attain true health and order and peace. It is said, sometimes, that poverty and disease and wretchedness are inevitable and even necessary, and therefore, in a sense, normal in human society. But surely this is as mistaken as it would be to say that the defects of disposition and temper, and even the positive sins, that mark many a Christian man are necessary and normal. Jesus came to save the unit, the individual man, from his sins; but he came also to save the sum, the body of which the individual is a member, from its sins. Failure to see this truth, that the divine purpose in the Christ is organic and comprehensive, as well as personal and individual, has often made Christians obstructive of social reform, or at least has made them lethargic and neglectful of their duty. They have limited the work of Christ to an individual redemption which affects condition rather than character, and which has its main, and often its only appreciable, result in eternity, delimited from time by a final and universal judgment day; while for the evil and disorder of the present they have sought a certain compensation in a future heaven. But the true heaven is the blossom and fruitage of earth; it is the harmony and crescendo of chords awakened in time; it is "the perfect round" of "the broken arcs" that are slowly shaping here.

The problem of the salvation of the world is all essentially in the problem of the salvation of a single soul, and the single unfolded and spiritualized man is the prophecy and pledge of "the new heaven and the new earth." All the progress of mankind is but fulfilment of God's purpose personally revealed in Jesus Christ.

See how Jesus has touched and changed society by his experience and work, and by the force of his personality even more than by his teachings. As the Baby of Bethlehem he has consecrated infancy. As the Child of Mary he has consecrated womanhood and maternity. As the Son of Man, embodying the divine thought and love in a life that is utterly divine, without losing one trait or element of its perfect humanness, he has raised the world's ideal of character and given a new law to human society. His self-sacrifice was no mere dramatic display, but a practical application of the law of love, which has made the cross the perpetual symbol of the glory and the invincible power of love. Slowly men are learning this law and the meaning of the cross. Life is not meant to be a perpetual strife and mutually hurtful competition, but a fellowship, a mutual service, a strife for one another instead of a strife against one another. The meaning of Jesus' life and work, of his teaching and his cross, must penetrate the industrial realm and shape the formulas of the market as completely as it must shape the formulas of theology. Indeed, its power will be efficacious in the former as fast as it is really efficacious in the latter. A selfish commerce has always had its strongest ally in a selfish theology.

The good-will that is native to the season is both typical and prophetic. The Christmas spirit in its purity must circle the year. Children sometimes wish it were "always Christmas"; they are unconscious prophets. As the embodied truth and righteousness and love of God, Jesus has given society an ideal of life which can be realized only through the regeneration of men and the realization of the law of love in all their mutual relations.

When we consider our individual condition, and perceive that to Jesus Christ we are indebted for our personal sense of divine mercy and forgiveness and help and guidance, — in a word, for the personal salvation which is begun and carried on toward completion through our contact with God in him; when we think of the hopes and aspirations and motives that have been awakened in our hearts by him; when the meaning and glory of the true life shines upon us as the revelation and gift of the Son of God, — we have some just conception of what we owe to him, and we begin to understand why we are moved to celebrate the Christmas festival.

When we reflect on what Jesus has done and is doing for society — for the home, for parents and children, for the great social body in all its functions and internal relations, for the oppressed, the poor, the miserable, and the dying; and when we think of the promise of social good that there is in his teachings, — a promise which will attain fulfilment as fast as these teachings become daily, practical principles in the business and pleasures and politics of men, — then we begin to see why Christendom should observe the Christmas festival.

The world is unspeakably better because that Baby smiled in the manger at Bethlehem. Life is more humane, and richer in hope, because

> "The Word had breath, and wrought
> With human hands the creed of creeds
> In loveliness of perfect deeds
> More strong than all poetic thought."

The burden and sorrow of life are lighter because the "Man of Sorrows bore our sins in his own body on the tree." We have hope and heart to face life's blackest hours, and fight manfully its fiercest battles with doubt and wrong, because Jesus lived and labored and suffered, and stood fast in love's sweet intent, thus demonstrating the presence of God in his world, and the reality of his love and care for us his weaker children.

We have hope and heart to confront death's solemn mystery because Jesus died and rose again from the dead. We have faith and comfort in God because he who came forth from the bosom of God has shown us God's heart. What have we not of good that is not bound up with the personality and life and thought of Jesus our Lord? Oh, to be followers of him! To be humble learners of his truth! To drink in his spirit! To know him and the power of his resurrection, and to yield all our life to his blessed rule! This is the true Christmas joy. And to give ourselves to his service, and so to give ourselves to humanity and to God, this is the true and priceless Christmas gift.

V.

SAVING OTHERS AND SAVING SELF.

THROUGH aisles of long-drawn centuries
  My spirit walks in thought,
And to that symbol lifts its eyes
  Which God's own pity wrought;
From Calvary shines the altar's gleam,
  The Church's East is there;
The Ages one great Minster seem,
  That throbs with praise and prayer.

And all the way from Calvary down
  The carven pavement shows
Their graves who won the martyr's crown,
  And safe in God repose;
The saints of many a warring creed
  Who now in heaven have learned
That all paths to the Father lead
  Where Self the feet have spurned.
                    JAMES RUSSELL LOWELL.

V.

SAVING OTHERS AND SAVING SELF.

And they that passed by railed on him, wagging their heads, and saying, "Ah, thou that destroyest the temple, and buildest it in three days, save thyself, and come down from the cross. Likewise also the chief priests, mocking, said among themselves, with the scribes, he saved others; himself he cannot save. — MARK xv. 29–31.

THIS is my text: "He saved others; himself he cannot save." These words from the lips of the priests were a bitter jibe flung in the face of the dying Christ. They expressed at once the hate, the sense of triumph, and the scorn, of men of whose security and peace, as they felt, the death of Jesus was the price. These words expressed also the judgment of the priests on Jesus' mad and now seemingly ruined enterprise. We who look back on that tragic event, as it lies in the strong interpretative light of Christian history, see how cruel and causeless was their hate, how empty and short-lived was their triumph, and how idle was their scorn. They have remembrance among men now, only because of the bad eminence given to them by their crime. They have an earthly immortality, only as their diabolical passions furnish the dark background to the glory which radiated from their victim and transfigured into imperishable beauty even the shameful cross. The long result of Calvary has at last wrung from the reluctant lips of the world a confession of Christ's great royalty.

But while we see, with some clearness of vision, the true character of those who crucified Jesus, we have not yet come, except imperfectly, and at rare moments, to a true perception of the deep error which lay at the heart of the priests' judgment on Christ's mission. That judgment they put into words when they said: "He saved others; himself he cannot save." The latter clause of this sentence is capable of a rendering which, while not changing its essential meaning, gives it fresh force as an expression of what the priests and scribes felt. "He saved others; cannot he save himself?" In this rendering the sneer is more apparent, while the nature of the judgment which prompts and points the sneer is quite as clearly manifest. How they pour contempt on this Galilean teacher who has attempted the overthrow of established institutions and ways of thinking, and habits and principles of conduct! What a pitiable spectacle he presents now, hanging there marred and helpless and dying on the execrated cross, framed in between redhanded outlaws! They might even pity him, now that he is safe in their clutches, did not his failure too deeply stir their contempt.

The real nature of their judgment upon the mission of Jesus will appear as we seek to analyze it. Unconsciously the priests, meaning only to sneer and condemn, uttered a great and vital truth. Unwittingly wicked men are sometimes prophets of God's purpose. In a consultation of Pharisees and priests as to how they might put Jesus to death, Caiaphas had said: " It is expedient for us that one man should die for the people," not knowing how true his words were in a far higher sense than he meant. A little later the Pharisees declared in wrath, as they saw the multitude — the fickle multitude — flocking after Jesus: " Behold, the world is gone after him," not thinking that in future ages their words would have a marvellous fulfilment.

So now, when the purpose of those who hate Jesus seems accomplished, and the perpetrators of the great crime stand mocking around the cross, the edge of their sarcasm is turned against themselves, though they know it not, and their judgment on Christ's mission becomes a judgment on their own sin.

" He saved others; himself he cannot save," — the priests were right; not as they thought, but in a far higher sense, Jesus could not save himself. If they meant, " He saved others from death " (alluding possibly to the raising of Lazarus a few days before), " himself he cannot save from death," they spoke truly, though their idea of his inability to save himself was hopelessly astray. If they meant, "He professed to save others from sorrow and sin; he cannot even save himself from pain and death," then also they spoke truly. Of course they did not think that Christ's inability to save himself was any other than natural, mainly physical, inability. They did not know that Christ's very inability to save himself from the cross was proof and manifestation of a higher power and a more colossal greatness than any of which they dreamed. The real point of their sneer lay in this, that they looked upon Christ as having failed, and saw in his failure their own triumph. More than that, they saw in his failure the proof of his weakness and folly. It was partly his crime that he had not succeeded. Often in the judgment of men simple failure carries with it the evidence that failure is deserved. Success, even in an enterprise of doubtful character, almost always, for the time being, justifies itself to the world. Success is a god which has a high place in the world's pantheon. The saying, "Nothing succeeds like success," is an expression of the involuntary tribute which men pay to the seeming effectiveness of to-day, before to-morrow comes with its inevitable rectification of false judgment. The successful man, as the contemporaneous world measures success, is the man who has followers and flatterers without number. It was the seeming success of the priests that turned the head of the fickle, impressionable multitude, and evoked the cry of execration against Jesus from the lips of some who, but the day before, had chanted his praise.

There was a representative worldly wisdom in the judgment of the priests. From their point of view, Jesus of Nazareth had set himself up as the Messiah and the Son of God, and had failed to fulfil any part of their Messianic ideal. His opposition to them was an unpardonable sin. Now he is condemned by the Sanhedrim, and executed by Roman soldiers under the order of the Procurator, and the would-be Messiah is thrust into company with thieves, that their infamy may over-lap him and deepen his degradation. They hate him because they recognize in him an enemy to their principles and power. They despise him as one who has been on a fool's errand and has justly come to grief.

And from the mere worldly point of view the priests were right. From that point of view Jesus had failed, had suffered defeat, and was expiating his stupendous blunder on the cross.

But while we are looking into the nature and ground of the priests' judgment on Christ, we see that very judgment transmuted into a thunderbolt which smites them, and, ere it smites, by its flash reveals their irremediable folly and their inexpiable guilt. "He saved others; himself he cannot save,"—this a sign of failure, an evidence of defeat, a ground of condemnation? It is the very apex of his triumph; it blazons his success; it crowns him with unfading glory. He proves himself the Christ, in that, saving others, he does not save himself. The courtier-priest, the surpliced worldling, counts the saving of self the supreme business of life, and so he sneers at the martyr who lays down his life for a sentiment. And God's word declares, and history affirms, and at last every human soul confesses, that he that saves himself is lost.

Jesus was not in the world to save himself. "For the Son of Man came not to be ministered unto, but to minister, and to give his life a ransom for many." He came to save men. For the attainment of this end he cheerfully accepted all the pain and cost of his mission, and yielded himself even to the death of the cross. He hungered for the salvation of souls from the impotence and wretchedness and guiltiness of sin; therefore he could not save himself. Saving himself was no part of his purpose.

It is evident to one who has a just conception of Christ's spirit and purpose that he could not save himself because he was perfectly under the sway and consecration of love. To avoid the very conditions by which alone love's purpose could be fulfilled, would be not to save, but to deny and defeat his true self; for he and love were one. He loved too well not to suffer; too faithfully not to die. He was under necessity, but that necessity was not material; the force that urged him to toil and endure and serve, that set his face steadfastly toward the crisis of Passion Week, and impelled him at last to hasten to the cross, was not external to him: it was the irresistible divine impulse of his own capacious and eager heart. All of his earthly life was an exhibition of love, that rose to a supreme exposure on Calvary. So great was his love, so lofty, so pure, so divine, that it seized upon the cross, an abhorred instrument of death, anointed with infamy and steeped in shame, and transformed it into a perpetual emblem of itself. Once the cross meant all of guilt and degradation that men could condense into a symbol; now it means love that passeth understanding. The grimness has all gone out of it, and in place thereof is a tender beauty. No more does it express cruel pain and languishing, but, instead, a "soft strength" that clasps the world to the heart of infinite goodness.

What a wonderful transformation is this! Has history its parallel? The executioner's sword smote off the head of a saintly Paul, but is there any beauty to men now in that weapon's cold glitter? The stake upheld John Huss amid the roaring flames of martyrdom, but is the stake henceforth winsome? The guillotine sheared off the head of many a heroine of whom the world was not worthy, but has that engine of death taken on any dear and tender symbolism? But the cross of Christ, rude wood and iron though it was, was sublimed by the love and greatness of him who hung thereon, and has become for all time, for all eternity, a spiritual fact and a spiritual power. Well may the Christian poet sing:

> " In the cross of Christ I glory;
> Towering o'er the wrecks of time,
> All the light of sacred story
> Gathers round its head sublime."

We talk about the love of Christ in words that vainly strive to bear the burden of its vast meaning. We endeavor to illustrate it from the shining deeds of human heroism; but our best illustrations are faint shadows of the "love of God which is in Christ Jesus our Lord." The mother sacrificing herself for her child, — as that mother in New Hampshire, who, in the dead of winter and far from help, wrapped her last garment about her baby, and, when late rescue came, lay a stiffened corpse, while the baby smiled an unconscious welcome in the rescuer's face; the patriot, — some Arnold von Winkelried, gathering into his own breast a sheaf of Austrian spears and bathing their pitiless points in his warm blood, while his countrymen of the Alps find a way to liberty through the broken wall of the hostile phalanx; the friend, — some Pythias, mounting the gallows with tranquil smile in place of his condemned and delaying Damon, — these, and countless other examples of love triumphing over fear and death, the gems that shine undimmed amid the murk of wonted human selfishness, help our thoughts as we strive to grasp the greatness of Jesus' love: but all these pale like stars about the glorious sun, when we look at the cross. In this supreme act of Christ's, — his voluntary submission to death for the salvation of men, — this act so natural to Christ and so vividly showing the culmination of his whole life's movement, we have embodied a root principle of holy life. It is the inability of love to save itself, to think of itself, to do anything but give itself for the blessing of its object. This is the nature of love. No pain deters it, for it quenches pain in the fountain of its own life. No cost bankrupts it, for it lives by self-expenditure. No danger appals it, for it fears naught but want of opportunity to exercise its sweet ministry. No extremity can exhaust it, for its supply is the unsounded, unmeasured sea of God's heart. Its name is God, for God is love.

The priests, looking upon Jesus, said: "He saved others; himself he cannot save," and knew not that love never saves itself, — that it is love's dearest privilege and highest joy to lavish itself in an unwasting stream of self-sacrifice. They thought he had failed, and knew not that the seeming failure was love's triumph. They looked upon him as their victim, and knew not that he, in dying by man's hand, was yet dying for man, and so was man's victor and sin's victor. They saw only the superficial fact from the world's low point of view, and had no glimmer of the truth that the death of Jesus in its spiritual meaning was the supreme revelation of God's redeeming love to man, and in its spiritual energy was God's power that is surely to possess and transform the world and determine the destiny of men and empires. They saw only with the eye of pride and selfishness and lust of earthly power; and seeing thus, they said: "His work was vain; his enterprise has failed; we have conquered an enemy to our influence and peace; let him be forgotten." As they saw, so sees the carnal mind always. The priests had no conception of the divine, redemptive significance of Christ's death. Of that they were not capable. Equally blind were they to its meaning as an exhibition of that spirit of love and self-sacrifice which can suffer and die for what the world calls a sentiment.

Calvary is a place of sharp contrasts. Evil looks never so evil as when seen side by side with goodness. Selfishness never shows so hideous a face as when surprised in some moment of keen antagonism to love. Human sin looks not so black in the lightning blaze of Sinai as it does in the soft splendor of the cross.

Calvary is also a place of wonderful revelations. God is there, in his suffering Son, exposing his heart to an insensible world. And man is there, showing the deep depravation of his moral nature by selfishness. What a revelation of sin does the cross give us! What blindness enwraps the soul that could see no beauty in the Christ! What malice directs the hand that could buffet his gentle face! What madness of rage enflames the heart that could pour out scorn and contumely upon his pain! There, on Calvary, is hung up a mirror that no resentful art can ever hide, in which, through all time, the sinful soul may see its own face. In those mocking priests and scribes was incarnate the spirit of selfishness that pervades the world, as in Christ was incarnate the spirit of divine love that seeks the world's redemption.

From that scene come beams of strong interpretative light upon the life of to-day. The judgment of the selfish world coincides with the judgment of the priests; though of many and various forms, in essential quality it is one with theirs. And just here, in this truth, is a lesson of immense practical import. The world cares supremely for itself. Sin is selfishness, and selfishness and Christlikeness, selfishness and love, are the opposite poles of moral quality. At one extreme is God, and at the other extreme is that personification of evil which the Bible calls Satan. As we are really under the dominion of love on the one hand, or of selfishness on the other, we are gravitating toward this extreme or that, approaching the divine or the Satanic. But the world does not believe that it is selfish, and in dire need of being broken on the cross of self-denial. The worldly spirit believes in itself as prudent and forehanded. Its main end is itself. It seeks its own comfort, its own advancement, and its own gain. The world calls the earnestness of the philanthropist folly, and looks with ill-concealed contempt on the missionary who buries his life in pagan lands that he may win the heathen to God. Certain forms of benevolence it smiles upon complacently, because some forms of benevolence are profitable; they bring an appreciable gain of praise or influence. But the martyr it cannot understand; the soul that flings itself with utter abandon into the weltering sea of human wretchedness, careless of praise or blame, seeking only at any cost the salvation of the lost, is to the world an insoluble enigma. It calls love a sentiment, and sneers at sentiment. It would call holy Stephen a poor fool, and bid him hold his peace, leave off preaching, and go into some trade that would bring him gold instead of smiting stones. When not opposed, it is contemptuous; when challenged, it hates.

The selfish heart sees Howard giving fortune and life to the service of the sick and the imprisoned, and at last dying of disease into the contagious atmosphere of which divine pity had urged him, and unconsciously it repeats the saying of the priests, "He saved others; himself he could not save." It looks upon some delicate woman spending her week-days in toil for bread, and her Sundays in unsparing devotion to comforting the children of sorrow and teaching them the gospel of Christ, and scornfully pities her self-sacrifice. Expenditure without gain that is palpable to sense it counts a form of prodigality that is to be avoided, if not condemned.

In many a Christian heart selfishness still contests with love the place of eminent influence. How often we are unconsciously moved by selfishness in the daily adjustment of our lives to those about us. The word of Christ urges us to loving service for others, and the example of Christ invites us to imitation; yet how slowly do we come under the control of his spirit. It costs to help others, to save others, to relax for them the stringent tyranny of want, and to lighten the oppression of care and sorrow. It costs to give them the real gospel of Christ. It costs to do good in any deep, large way. It demands hours of work, often wearisome work, when personal ends claim all our energy. It makes frequent invasion on mere physical comfort. It calls for the perpetual exercise of sympathy, and sympathy is often painful. Many a man avoids the sight of suffering from a mere selfish reluctance to have his placidity of feeling disturbed. Many will not think of the griefs and famishment of those about them because the thought is troublesome.

Moreover, a real Christlike service contravenes

those false ideas, which we so often cherish as true, of personal development and advancement. How often culture is selfish, and the desire for it a selfish passion. Large claims are made upon us continually for benevolent work, such as teaching the ignorant, guiding the weak, and persuading the wanderer back to the paths of virtue. In the church, in the Sunday school, and in society are needy and inviting fields for Christian labor. "But," say some, "I cannot engage in this work; it is too exacting. I need my time for myself. I must rest, I must read, I must care for myself, or I shall fail of that mental growth which I ought to attain. I cannot afford to give the one day in the week when there is respite from business cares to the service of others, and so neglect myself." Many a Christian has beguiled himself into thinking, with a kind of stiff conscientiousness, that he ought to give all the hours of the Lord's day wholly to himself. Does it not occur to you, my friends, that some time for self-culture may be, and ought to be, rescued from the tyrannous demands of business; that a man has no right to make himself a slave of business; that the gain of such slavery is not worth its cost even now, and will be still less so by and by? Is it not plain, too, that culture secured at the expense of Christlikeness is not the culture that you most need, and that it is too dear at such a price? The end of life is not merely knowledge, power and possession, but character, manhood; and indeed character is these — knowledge, possession, and power — in highest form. The faithful missionary, the self-sacrificing Sunday-school teacher, the man or woman who is never too busy to give thought and time and money and toil for the comfort and encouragement and salvation of others, is winning a richer culture and ripening a nobler character than is possible to the selfish soul, however great may be his learning or his art. Let us get knowledge with all eagerness; but if we seek it at the expense of that which is higher, we are rebuked even by the pagan Confucius, who said: "Knowledge is to know all men; benevolence is to love all men."

Which is the true exemplar of the best life, — the priest who so feared the loss of prestige and power that he must bring even Jesus to the cross, or Jesus who dies for love of the world and is mocked with the cry: "He saved others; himself he cannot save"? If, as you look on this scene, Jesus alone is beautiful and glorious to you, then remember that if you would be like him, if you would save others, you cannot save yourself; you neither can save yourself, nor will you care to save yourself, from toil and cost and pain. You will forget yourself. You will lose yourself in the abandon of generous, serviceful, Christlike life. And then, as Jesus found a heavenly joy and an enduring triumph even in the cross, so you, losing yourself in his spirit and for him, will find the same joy and share in the same triumph. So, at last, saving others, you will find yourself saved, having, with your Lord, "endured the cross, despising the shame," and entered into the joy of a heavenly power and a heavenly peace.

"Speak, History, who are life's victors? Unroll thy long
annals, and say —
Are they those whom the world called the victors, who won
the success of a day?
The Martyrs, or Nero? The Spartans who fell at Thermopylæ's tryst,
Or the Persians and Xerxes? His judges, or Socrates?
Pilate or Christ?"

And now, as I close, I am burdened with the thought that, to many, the highest attainments of human goodness set forth in the Scriptures and personalized in Christ are beautiful but impracticable dreams. But it is only in their moments of lowest spiritual sensibility that this can be so to any who have really felt the beauty and power of the Son of God. The love of Christ, as the pervasive atmosphere of a life in the world, has in it so great a suggestion of unreality and unattainableness, because there is still so much of selfishness in our hearts. The wisdom of the world counts it needful that every life should have in it at least a little salt of selfishness, and the spirit of the world prevails with us. But not so have we learned of Christ. Godliness is not impracticable, even in the midst of " a crooked and perverse generation ; " nor is it only a beautiful ideal toward which we shall rise in our songs and our prayers, but which perforce must be forgotten in the rough, wrestling life of every day. Christlikeness is not mysticism; it is "love, joy, peace, long-suffering, gentleness, goodness, faith, meekness, temperance;" it is loving God with all the heart, mind, soul, and strength, and our neighbor as ourselves; it is having fellowship with Christ day by day, and doing each day's work with hearts instructed by him, and eyes that trace out his footsteps, and feet that press the prints of his feet as " he went about doing good."

And on the threshold of this beautiful life are written in letters of gold the words : " If any man will come after me, let him deny himself, and take up his cross, and follow me."

> "God the Father give us grace
> To walk in the light of Jesus' Face;
> God the Son give us part
> In the hiding-place of Jesus' heart;
> God the Spirit so hold us up
> That we may drink of Jesus' cup!"

Now unto the King eternal, immortal, invisible, the only wise God, be honor and glory, through Jesus Christ, for ever and ever. Amen.

VI.

THE MIND OF CHRIST.

I WENT to seek for Christ,

. . . . . .

And in a hovel rude,
With naught to fence the weather from his head,
　The King I sought for meekly stood;
　　A naked, hungry child
　　Clung round his gracious knee,
And a poor hunted slave looked up and smiled
　To bless the smile that set him free;
New miracles I saw his presence do, —
　No more I knew the hovel bare and poor,
The gathered chips into a wood-pile grew,
　The broken morsel swelled to goodly store;
I knelt and wept: my Christ no more I seek,
His throne is with the outcast and the weak.

　　　　　　　　JAMES RUSSELL LOWELL.

VI.

THE MIND OF CHRIST.

Let this mind be in you, which was also in Christ Jesus. — PHIL. ii. 5.

IN the notable passage from St. Paul's letter to the Philippians, extending from the fifth to the eleventh verses of the second chapter, the dominant thought of the apostle is the humility and self-subjection of Jesus contrasted with his consequent divine exaltation. He, the Son of God, "emptied himself, taking the form of a bond-servant. . . . Wherefore God also highly exalted him, and gave unto him the name which is above every name." The exaltation is because of the humiliation, yet it is also through the humiliation. Even in his subjection Jesus achieves his exaltation, and the words, "Wherefore God also highly exalted him," express the objective fulfilment of the subjective process through which the Great Servant rises into manifest sovereignty. The sovereignty before which every knee shall bow, and to which every tongue shall render willing homage, is the sovereignty of love, self-sacrifice, and service. These are the great elements of "the mind which was in Christ Jesus." This is the "mind" of which the apostle says to the Philippians: "Let this mind be in you." The experience and spirit of Jesus are cited as eminent, but not singular. That is, here, in Jesus, are disclosed the true spirit, aim, and process of human life. Humility, love, service, — these are the steps to greatness of work and character. The experience of Jesus is not abnormal, but normal; it furnishes the norm or standard toward which we are to strive. The cross, with its accompanying shame and suffering and death, is the sign rather than the measure of Jesus' self-subjection to love's behests; the service is limited only by the capacity to serve, and love meets no cost that it will not gladly pay. This is a strenuous doctrine of life, but it is the true doctrine. Let us look at it a little more closely. "Let this mind be in you which was also in Christ Jesus." The word "mind" ($\phi\rho\text{ονεῖτε}$) implies more than the action of intelligence: it includes also feeling and purpose. It means this way of looking at life, this sort of feeling toward men, and this kind of purpose in action. As Jesus thought, felt, and purposed, so do ye. In a word, have the mind, the heart, the aim of Jesus Christ. These words strike the key-note of the highest human life; they suggest the ideal toward which the followers of Christ should aspire and strive.

This mind is (1) *a mind of love.* Jesus was not

carrying out a pre-arranged and formal scheme. There is little likeness in him to the artificial functionary of theology. He was born into the world and into the race, flesh of man's flesh, and bone of man's bone, and nature of man's nature. In him God revealed himself in forms of genuine human feeling and action and character. In him was revealed also the divine kinship and possibilities of man. Jesus was the Son of Man; therefore he understood man, and felt for man in real and natural human ways. He was the Son of God; therefore he thought about man and felt toward man in true, divine ways. Unfettered by the littleness of neighborhood, the narrowness of sect, and the selfishness of tribe or race, he loved men with the fulness and greatness of his own great nature. He loved men, not merely an abstract conception called mankind. This love disclosed itself in quick and unerring sympathy with men in their needs, their weaknesses, their aspirations, their sorrows, and their joys. Accidents of condition and culture put no bar on his sympathy. He lived and labored most among the poor, but he loved also the rich. He was seen most often with the lowly, but he did not shun the proud and mighty. He was disconcerted no more by the haughtiness and resentfulness of the cultured than he was by the ingratitude and fickleness of the ignorant and frivolous. He loved humanity, and each concrete individual furnished object and opportunity for the exercise of his sympathy. His love disclosed itself in his appreciation of persons. The individual was significant to him, not simply as one of a number, an atom of the mass, but as a unique personality, with individual needs, aptitudes and capacity. The woman that was a sinner, Simon the scornful Pharisee, Peter the impulsive disciple, Judas the traitor, the officious and bustling Martha, the contemplative, affectionate Mary, the slow-witted, incredulous Thomas, the politic Nicodemus, the querulous cripple by the pool, the ambitious mother of James and John, — each was understood, appreciated, and dealt with by Jesus with unerring judgment of each individual's nature and needs.

His love disclosed itself also in his patience. The temptation to be impatient is one of the strongest temptations which the far-seeing and benevolent soul has to meet. Men do not readily respond, either individually or in the mass, to spiritual influence. He who would save men must have an invincible faith in their salvability, and an invincible patience in waiting for the slow processes of spiritual development. How disappointing the world must have been to the prophet of Nazareth, who came into Judea pressed in spirit to preach " the kingdom of God" and to lead men into it! How sluggish and even antipathetic was most of the life about him! Even the most docile disciples, by their inaptitude and obtuseness to spiritual ideas and motives, wrung from the heart of Jesus more than once the cry, "O foolish ones, and slow of heart to understand!"

But Jesus was impatient only with knowing and selfish hypocrisy. At the one point of his contact with the spirit of diabolical selfishness masquerading under the garb of religion, his feeling kindled into a flame of indignation. There was no passion, in the coarse sense of ordinary human anger, but there was the wrath of outraged love against that which denied love and sought to destroy it in the name of Him who is love. Jesus was patient with the impulsive and with the dull; patient with weakness and with misguided strength; patient with folly and with fault. Stronger than every revulsion of feeling from the grossness and badness, of which there was so much in the life about him, was his love for the men who, beneath the grossness and the badness, had the capacity for being sons of God.

The mind of Jesus was (2) *a mind of self-sacrifice.* That is, the love of Jesus was not merely a sentiment or state of feeling; it poured itself forth in action that was marked by prompt and continuous self-sacrifice. His life literally fulfilled his words: "The Son of Man came not to be ministered unto, but to minister, and to give his life a ransom for many."

Nothing but the cross is an adequate, or even tolerable, symbol of that life. He died for the world, but his death was only the culmination of a prolonged self-subjection to the one end of saving men through the revelation of God and the manifestation of all-suffering love.

The measure of Christ's self-sacrifice was the capacity of man to receive good as the result of that self-sacrifice, — not, indeed, man's immediate, but his ultimate capacity. True self-sacrifice is not aimless, nor wasteful. In itself it has no merit. The madman hurls himself from the precipice, or rushes into the fire, and his action is as aimless and as worthless as a hurricane or a conflagration. The patriot flings himself upon the advancing bayonets of the enemy, and the martyr walks, singing, to the stake; but the one purchases by his blood the freedom of his country, and the other, by his costly testimony, vindicates and perpetuates the faith, that, by and by, blesses all men. Self-sacrifice with a moral motive is always fruitful, and justifies itself in the large economy of life. The self-sacrifice of Jesus was the price which love freely paid for the attainment of its beneficent ends. The measure of that self-sacrifice is not to be found in its immediate result, nor even in all the results which history thus far gives us, but in the possibility of man to attain the fulness of being and power and experience as a child of God. "For the joy that was set before him, Jesus endured the cross, despising the shame." We must take into account the whole spiritual destiny of man in order to get the measure of Jesus' self-sacrifice; that is, his self-sacrifice expressed the entire reach, both of his love for man and his thought of man, and of the fulfilled divine purpose in man.

The mind of Jesus was (3) *a mind of service*. Jesus did not seek merely the one end of expiating sin, and thus warding off penalty from the sinner. The truth underlying this crude conception is often lost in the gross and immoral caricature of both God and man, of which theology has been sometimes ignorantly guilty. Whatever he may have had to do with sin, as a formal transaction affecting man's forensic standing before the Supreme Judge, Jesus had mainly and constantly to do with sin as a condition of human defect, perversion, and incapacity. Salvation is the conquest of sin through the awakening of spiritual life in man's heart, the extrusion of evil by the power of indwelling divine affections and motives, and the discipline of the soul in knowledge, righteousness, and love. The process is vital, and is accomplished by the vital force of the divine life in man, imparted by the continuous touch of a divine personality. Hence the relation of Jesus to men is a relation of genetic and formative influence. Jesus is supremely the servant. He serves in his life, his deeds, his teaching, his example, his death, his resurrection, and the continuous play of his unmeasured spiritual influence on humanity. His public ministry on earth is typical and revelatory. "He went about doing good," — thus simply is expressed the essential quality of his unique and majestic life. His great idea, uttered and illustrated in manifold forms, identifies the service of God with the service of man. In his life, idea and fact continuously and completely correspond. The world has had many benefactors, — many men and women who have thought and toiled and suffered for the good of their fellow-creatures; but in range and fulness and elevation of service, Jesus stands as entirely alone as he stands alone in perfectness of character.

Here is the pattern of human life. We can look to no one else without disapointment. In him alone do we find the ever enticing, ever approached, yet ever unattained, ideal. The service which Jesus renders to man meets not one crisis of man's need, but every crisis. It includes in its circle the whole man, — not only the whole individual, but the whole organic life of the race. It does not exhaust itself at one period of time, but sweeps the entire course of man's existence. Historically and geographically, Jesus touched the world at a single point; but spiritually he puts himself in contact with the whole. There is no power of the human personality, whether it be of intelligence, or of feeling, or of will, to which he does not minister. There is no real interest of man which his beneficent purpose does not include. There is no essential need of the human spirit which he does not meet.

The Mind of Christ.

The fulness of Jesus' service to the world appears in this, — that while it was objective and palpable in his works of healing and help to the needy immediately about him in Palestine, its essential power and aim are subjective and spiritual. What he does for man is mainly wrought in man. He never pauses on the material, the surface of life, but reaches to the inmost centre and secret of human susceptibility. He aims not merely at relief, but at renovation; not merely at comfort, but at blessedness; not merely at a bettered condition, but at a redeemed and transfigured life. The supreme motive and aim co-ordinate all the varieties of action. The purpose to do good reaches far; it reaches to the absolute good of man in the fulfilment of his destiny as a son of God and a participator in the divine nature and glory.

This, then, is "the mind which was in Christ Jesus." It is the mind of love to all men, — a love that reaches below and beyond all accidents of condition and place and time; a love which, having its spring in the indwelling nature of God, rises into a pure and unquenchable "enthusiasm of humanity," and lifts every life which feels the pulse of its power up to the level of the divine. It is the mind of self-sacrifice, — a pure and self-less passion, that burns up selfishness in its holy flame, and makes of life one limitless capability of self-expenditure in the attainments of love's ends. It is a mind of service, — a disposition and purpose to do good that exalts every action into a manifestation and fulfilment of the good will of God.

In a word, it is the mind by which he whom it animates and informs, however humble may be his sphere and however small may be his means, is exalted into a helper and saviour of his fellowmen, and a bringer in of the kingdom of God.

This is the mind which we are urged to seek, taught how to attain, and divinely enabled to exert and illustrate in life.

As we turn our thought back for a moment to the plane of the struggling, selfish, and low-pitched life that we know, to which most of us are so closely confined that only in shining moments of thought and feeling are we clearly conscious of any other, we are prone to yield to the spirit of discouragement and doubt that rises within us. This is the ideal; we must believe that. We feel the strong enticement of the idea, or the dream, as we half involuntarily call it; but the pull of selfishness in our hearts and the gravitation of the materiality all about us are strong, and too often prevailing. Is this, then, only the rapturous thought of the seer and saint? Is there not rather the divinest practicality in the conception of life which Jesus brings before us? One of the great elements of power in the personal ministry of Jesus was his manifest and contagious belief in the worth and salvability of men. In a deep sense, because he believed so utterly in God, Jesus believed in man. The very extent of his requirements, and the very loftiness of his teachings, witness to his vast faith in man's possibility. That he should say, " Be ye perfect, even as your Father who is in heaven is perfect," when once we really grasp the meaning of the words, thrills our hearts with hope and the aspiration to reach upwards and strive to prove our sonship to God.

It is not then a mere dream of an unattainable power and excellence which exhales before us from the personality and communication of Jesus. The exhortation is positive and forceful. It comes to all who will see and hear.

Listen to these words, — not mine, but St. Paul's, not St. Paul's, but Christ's, — listen, and grasp the meaning which, through these words, the Spirit discloses to you : Let this mind, this great mind of love and self-sacrifice and service, this mind which was in Christ Jesus, be in you. It does not matter what your occupation may be, nor the apparent extent of your sphere, nor the measure of your specific capability as a worker. This exhortation is not for the few, but for all who will live toward the best. The humblest life gives ample scope for exhibiting and exercising the mind of Christ. What was Judea to the world? What is your little sphere to the broad expanse of human life? Geographically, Judea was but a point on the surface of the habitable globe. But life is not measured by geographical boundaries. The narrow circle of which you are the centre is a sufficient arena for achieving life's greatest work, and winning the soul's grandest victories. Each personality is the centre of the universe. Each human soul is the temple and throne of God. Each man or woman may live with a truth and force and beauty that will be enduring and fruitful through all eternity. You may fail of attaining riches; you may not win eminence on the roll of temporal fame; but you can possess the mind of the Son of God; you can live in his spirit; you can work with his force; you can testify with his truth; you can love with his heart; and you can rise daily toward heaven with his aspiration. You may barely win the livelihood which is comprised in food and clothes and means to move about on the earth; but meanwhile you can abundantly live, a blessing and a help to your fellows and a shining witness to the presence of God in the hearts and homes of men.

In conclusion, two thoughts claim our attention. These are: 1. The influence of "the mind of Christ" on the work which we do. "The mind of Christ" makes all effort terminate (1) not on the reward, that is, on the mere wage which men pay for our service. A fair return for honest work is a just and necessary element in the economic relations of men. Very few people, comparatively, get their living at first hand from nature. The material return which society renders to each individual in compensation for labor of hand or brain is a part of the mutual service by which men nourish and sustain each other. Industry of every sort is entitled to its appropriate fruits. As all workers contribute to the material or moral wealth of the community, so all rightfully share in the material products by which bodily life is supported. But the end of work is not material. He who toils only for money, or its equivalent, has not yet risen to any true conception of the moral life, — that is, the real life of man.

(2) Nor does effort inspired and directed by " the mind of Christ" terminate on the thing done. It is not for the sake of the harvest that is gathered, or the machine that is invented, or the house that is built, or the garment that is manufactured, or the book that is written, or the picture that is painted, or the statue that is carved, that the true human worker puts forth his best energies. There is an honest and noble pride in doing well whatever one does. In some sense a man puts himself into his work. Thomas Carlyle's sturdy father built stone bridges that incarnated his own strong intelligence and solid worth of character. Sleazy and superficial work is immoral. " Scamp carpentering," said Adam Bede, " is an abomination to God." The conscientious workman must absolve himself to himself. Apart from the price which his work brings, he recognizes a real value to himself and to society in putting excellence into

the thing which he does. It is a mean sort of dishonesty that one practises who does anything slightingly. Doing whatsoever we do as unto the Lord, is the form into which St. Paul puts his idea of manly and Christian industry. This includes much more than simply taking care to do well the task that is in hand, but it certainly includes that.

(3) But rightly inspired effort does not terminate merely on the excellence of the work. It rises higher and contemplates an end that coordinates all work with the noblest moral and spiritual enterprises. The mind of Christ makes all effort terminate on man, — on his comfort, his enlightenment, and his betterment. Thus all work, from the humblest to the highest tasks, takes on the form, because it has in it the essence, of true service. The house is built not simply for a price, nor simply for the sake of making a good house, but that there may be a home in which sweet human life may thrive and blossom and grow into beauty and power. The carpenter drives the nail not less surely, and fits the joint not less nicely, because his forecasting heart is happy with the thought of the enhanced human weal which he is helping to produce. The lesson is taught not simply for the fee, nor for the sake of good pedagogics and sound learning, but that there may be a higher measure and power of knowing, that is, a higher quality of intellectual life, in the pupil. The teacher is the benefactor, both of the indi-

vidual taught and of the society to which he belongs. By his work the level of intelligence is raised, and the world is helped onward in its moral development. The teaching will not be less accurate and broad because the teacher glows with the thought of what he is doing for humanity. The song is sung not that silvery notes may bring an increased supply of silver coin, nor even that a higher art may be attained and exhibited, but that the listener may have a pure pleasure, and with the pleasure may receive an inspiration and uplift of soul. The singer will not sing less sweetly because her heart swells with the glad thought of her ministry to the æsthetic and spiritual needs of men.

The spirit of Christ in us makes all our work noble, and fruitful to a degree far beyond the power of any economic standards to measure. It makes all work well-doing, or, in the expressive phrase of St. Paul, τὸ καλὸν ποιοῦντες, — "beautiful doing."

2. The influence of "the mind of Christ" on the worker.

A vital part of the result of all work is its effect on the worker. All our activity has a potent and permanent reflex influence. The nature of the reflex influence is determined by the motive of the action. We are bettered or worsened by whatever we voluntarily do. Herein we see the necessity of action to the discipline of character. The teachings of the New Testament make much of conduct, because through conduct principle becomes an effective force. What we are depends on what we do, as well as what we do depends on what we are. In childhood, if rightly taught, we acquire moral habits before we can grasp moral principles. So the development of man in intelligence and character demands action as well as contemplation and reflection. Action confirms as well as reveals purpose. The divine education of the human race luminously exhibits the truth that we are set to doing work not merely that work may be done, but that *we* may do it, and so derive the culture that can come only through the reflex of our activity. In all that we do we attain a result in quality and direction and force of life. Often the importance of work lies far more in its effect on us than in its immediate product. The world conceivably might get on without your specific contribution of industry; but *you* cannot get on without it.

The great business of life is not to do things, but to become something large and fair. As it is not the deed itself, but the motive, in which lies the moral character of the deed, so it is not the specific task that is done, but "the mind" with which it is done, that ennobles both deed and doer. Here is the central point of highest human fellowship, that fellowship into which all are invited, — the possibility, not of doing great things, but of doing all things greatly. The spirit of love ranks the feet-washing in that upper room in Jerusalem with the raising of Lazarus and the dying on the cross. The lowliest woman on a back street in this city may be the true kinswoman of Florence Nightingale in the Crimea. Moral affinities run across all barriers of race and culture and possession. Whosoever does the will of God is brother and sister and mother of the Lord. The modest teacher in the far West, or on an Asiatic mission-field, struggling against want and temptation and sorrow, may be so doing her work as to prove that she is of the blood-royal, and her spirit puts her endeavor on a level with his who bears on his heart the redemption of the world.

The significance of the parable of the idlers in the market-place is just this: The eleventh hour men receive the denarius equally with those who bore the heat and burden of the day, because motive counts; the spirit with which work is done counts; and the denarius is not reward, but expression of the equal co-partnership of all who labor with the true mind whenever and wherever opportunity comes. This soldier carried the flag to the top of the redoubt, and fell pierced to the heart; that soldier pressed on and received the surrendered sword of the vanquished commander; the first not less than the last is in the full fellowship of heroes and victors.

God measures our lives not by what we do, but by what we would do. The spirit is everything. "The mind which was in Christ Jesus" is the essential capability of the greatest service.

Receiving the inspirations and impulses of this

"mind," the soul grows great. The humblest worker attains a divinely attested nobility. The development of character is not dependent on the accidents or mere incidents of life. Whether station be high or low is relatively of little significance. God is at home everywhere, and the divine spirit domesticates himself in the lowliest life to make it glorious with the splendors of moral purpose and endeavor. Rank in this world is exclusive. Wealth is attainable by few. The aristocracy of blood, or of trade, or of letters, is difficult to enter. But *life*, the life of God, is open to all. There is no exclusive competition here. No one's gain in the sphere of the spirit is another's loss. All may enter into this fellowship, and all may win this prize. To enter into this fellowship is the true achievement. Life is possessed and fulfilled, not in work but in purpose and endeavor. He who loves and aspires and attempts, becomes the Christ, — the servant who, in serving, attains and discloses the only real sovereignty, that sovereignty to which every knee in heaven and on earth bows in willing homage.

The business of life, then, is *service*. The crown of life is *being*, — the Christ-like quality, the Christ-like power, the Christ-like joy. It does not matter what you do, so that while you live you serve. The secret of power to serve, in highest ways though it may be through humblest means, is the presence and potency in you of "the mind which was also in Christ Jesus."

VII.

THE ENTHUSIASM OF JESUS.

BREATHE on me, Breath of God,
   Fill me with life anew,
That I may love what thou dost love,
   And do what thou wouldst do.

Breathe on me, Breath of God,
   Until my heart is pure,
Until with thee I will one will,
   To do or to endure.

Breathe on me, Breath of God,
   Till I am wholly thine,
Till all this earthly part of me
   Glows with thy fire divine.

Breathe on me, Breath of God,
   So shall I never die,
But live with thee the perfect life
   Of thine eternity.

EDWIN HATCH.

VII.

THE ENTHUSIASM OF JESUS.

The zeal of thine house hath eaten me up. — JOHN ii. 17.

THESE words are quoted by the Evangelist from the Sixty-ninth Psalm, — a plaintive psalm that by some scholars has been ascribed to Jeremiah; by others it is referred to a later time. Evidently it is the work of a Hebrew who was involved in deep trouble because of his devotion to the house and service of Jehovah. His ardent piety had awakened, or had drawn to itself, fierce persecution. He exclaims, —

"For thy sake (O God of Israel) I have borne reproach,
Confusion hath covered my face.
I have become estranged from my brethren,
And an alien to my mother's sons.
For zeal for thine house hath consumed me,
And the reproaches of them that reproach thee have fallen
upon me." [1]

When, early in his ministry, Jesus entered the temple, and, in a noble rage at the desecration committed by greedy speculators who had invaded the house of prayer with their merchandise and

[1] Perowne's translation.

their chaffering, suddenly swept them all aside, over-turning their money-tables and driving out their cattle, the disciples, astonished beyond measure by his boldness, instinctively recalled these words of an old and familiar psalm as descriptive of their Master's mood. Long afterward, when St. John dictated to some sympathetic disciple the story of Jesus' ministry, his mind naturally reverted to the same words.

The prophet of Nazareth, like a true Israelite, cherished a deep reverence for the place where the nation worshipped God, and he glowed with holy indignation at the defilement of the sanctuary around which clustered the solemn memories and hallowed traditions of a great historic faith and service.

The fitness of the application of these words, "The zeal of thine house hath consumed me," to Jesus appears not only in the scene in the temple which St. John describes, but also in his entire public ministry. It is no perversion of the text to take it as expressive of a certain earnestness and intensity that marked his spirit and pervaded all his utterance and work.

No one can study sympathetically the life of Jesus without being impressed by his deep and continuous enthusiasm. There was in him nothing of the madness and volcanic fury that sometimes mark the action and speech of the reformer and the prophet of denunciation. Whatever view we

may take of his essential nature, whatever may be
the result of our attempt to classify him, — if we
are bold enough to make such an attempt, — every
one of us must confess that here is a soul whose
white light of transparent wisdom is tremulous
with the flame of a consuming zeal. Jesus was not
a peripatetic philosopher, calmly giving utterance
to wise maxims and polished epigrams. He certainly was calm; the poise of his judgment was as
steady as the penetration of his spiritual insight
was sure. But his calmness was never coldness.
His heart's red blood pulsated in all his speech, so
that one may say of his very style, as it appears in
the reports of the Evangelists, "It is vascular and
alive; cut these words, and they would bleed."
There was never a merely judicial or philosophical interest in his view of life; on the contrary,
there was always an intense human interest that
qualified every saying as surely as it qualified
every act of his ministry. He had not a theory
to inculcate, but a message to announce, and a
work to do. In the highest and holiest sense
of that great word, Jesus was an *apostle*, — one
sent of God. The world has long recognized
him as a teacher — a teacher on so high a plane
that he inevitably appropriates the title, *the teacher*,
in the domain of morals and religion. Every other
pure voice in this domain seems but a faint echo
of his voice. Moses, Confucius, Buddha, Zoro-
aster, Socrates, Epictetus, Marcus Aurelius, — it is

almost idle to suggest a comparison between him and them. We measure their elevation by the standard which he has furnished. But he was more than a teacher; so much more, indeed, that his teaching derives its mightiest force from his unique personality. His words, set to the divine melody of his life, are lifted to a new pitch of meaning, and thus command the ear and heart of men with an irresistible attraction, and an authority to which instinctively we bow, as if, in his speech, heaven and earth had suddenly become vocal. He heaves the ocean of human life in tides the sweep of which is measured only by the capability of the universal human heart to think and feel. "The sages and heroes of history," said Channing, "are receding from us, and history contracts the record of their deeds into a narrow and narrower page. But time has no power over the name and deeds and words of Jesus Christ." Other men who have been great forces in the life of the world find their true measure in the judgment of men at last. But Jesus, with every turn of the revolving planet, rises upon our view in more colossal proportions. We feel him in the realm of spiritual thought as we feel the elemental forces of nature in the realm of matter. He is diffused throughout our civilization as heat and light are diffused throughout the atmosphere. Yet every century makes him more intensely personal. A thousand times has critical thought analyzed his influence and defined his person, and a thousand times has he confronted critical thought anew with the still fascinating and unsolved problem. " He walked in Judea eighteen hundred years ago," wrote Carlyle; " his sphere-melody, flowing in wild native tones, took captive the ravished souls of men, and, being of a truth sphere-melody, still flows and sounds, though now with thousandfold accompaniments and rich symphonies, through all hearts, and modulates and divinely leads them."

The very closeness of Jesus to us, not lessened, but rather increased, by the lapse of eighteen centuries, makes it difficult for us to view him as he was when he walked in Judea and Galilee and gave his message to men. There is truth in the saying that the world has idealized the peasant teacher and prophet of Nazareth. Let it frankly be admitted. And what does that mean? That the original has been exaggerated and falsified? No; but that men have risen in power to apprehend the real Christ. It was they who saw him only as a peasant teacher who misconceived him. The idealizing process is a process of discovery. Our highest thought of Jesus to-day, as the Son of God, the universal man, the concrete revelation of God in and to humanity, is truer to the reality of what Jesus is than the thought of him conceived by any of his contemporaries.

St. Paul had advanced far beyond the disciples in spiritual apprehension when he said: "Yea, though we have known Christ after the flesh, yet know we him (after the flesh) no longer." The great apostle was approaching, if he had not already quite attained, the true interpretative point of view to which the entire Church is slowly but surely coming. So, when men say that the world has idealized Jesus of Nazareth, I say: Yes; the world must idealize the Jesus of Nazareth in order to see him as he is, — the Christ of humanity. What some are pleased to call a process of idealization is simply a process of discovery, — the result of growth in power of spiritual vision and comprehension. If we hold closely to the spiritual line, and to the clearly authenticated representations which he makes of himself, we shall be in no danger of arriving at an exaggerated estimate of Jesus; the chief danger always is in the opposite direction, — that of belittling him by our materialism.[1]

But it will aid us in apprehending the Christ in

[1] Long after these words were written, Alexander Balmain Bruce, D.D., in an address before the University of Chicago uttered these significant words : " Foremost in importance among the good omens [of the present time] is the intense desire of many among us to know the mind of the historic Jesus, and to give to it the authoritative place in the faith and life of the Church. Not a few of our best men, I fear, have been tempted in these years to get weary of ecclesiastical Christianity; but one rarely meets with a man who is weary of Christ. The appeal of malcontents is rather from the Church to Christ, from modern presentations of the Christian religion to the religion embodied in the authentic sayings of the Great Master. There is as little weari-

his relations to us of daily guidance and practical help, if we can get a clear view of him as the historical Christ. This for most of us is difficult, mainly because of our prejudices on the theological or anti-theological side.

It is a singular figure which the Evangelists present to us, — a Galilean peasant, without the laborious and technical learning of the Rabbinical schools, speaking the language of the common people, transcending as well as contradicting the current ideas of God and religion and ethics, and exercising an authority that startled his hearers by its neglect of appeal to the recognized standards, while it commanded them by its inherent, unhesitating imperativeness. As we study him in his original setting of race and political condition and religious institutions, there are many aspects both of his personality and of his teaching that strongly

---

ness of Jesus Christ as there is of nature, of the world revealed to us by the eye and the ear.

"After many disenchantments, multiplying with the years of our life, these two objects, Jesus and nature, retain their charm unabated, growing rather as old age steals on. What is true of the individual Christian is not less true of Christendom at large. It is going on to two millenniums since Christ was born, but that event, and the life it ushered in, are not losing their attraction through the long lapse of time. Rather Christ is being born anew amongst us; through scientific study, devout thought, and loving endeavor at imaginative realization, his life and ministry are being enacted over again, insomuch that it may be said with truth that the Hero of the gospel story is better known to day, and more intelligently estimated than he ever has been since the Christian era began."

solicit our attention. All these, for the present, I pass by, and ask you to consider for a few minutes that quality which has notable expression in the text, — his deep and unquenchable enthusiasm.

It is characteristic of our cool and critical time — a time in which we analyze our most sacred emotions with something of the nonchalance with which we analyze a flower or a muscle — that the very word enthusiasm, as well as the quality which it expresses, has fallen somewhat into contempt. That one is enthusiastic is sufficient evidence to many that he is weak or unwise. Some writers on the life of Jesus even have declared as proof of his limitation and defect that he was an enthusiast. But may not this contempt for enthusiasm be a proof rather of defect in those who indulge the contempt? The cynic scoffs at the gentle fervors of friendship. The misanthrope sneers at the impassioned utterance of human love. With all their learning and astuteness, — their encyclopædic sciences and multiform worldly wisdom, — how many have ice at their hearts, and what they call coolness of judgment is often the chill that attests the death of their holiest sentiments and purest passions.!

He alone reads history aright who sees that "every great and commanding movement in the annals of the world is the triumph of enthusiasm." Some one, in discussing a question of theology, — so solemn a question as that of future retribution,

— said: "Sentiment is ruled out of court." This sentence is tell-tale. When sentiment is ruled out of theology and enthusiasm out of life, what wonder that men ask: "Is life worth living?"

Yes, Jesus was an enthusiast. A divine passion glowed in his breast, and a divine ideal thrilled and enticed him. That divine passion was the infinite love of God which he not so much felt and expressed as embodied. He *was* the love of God become concrete and personal. The object of his love was humanity, and the whole significance and worth of humanity he saw represented in the individual soul. The philanthropist often regards the multitude at the expense of the individual; but in Jesus was such particularness joined with such universality of love, and such sanity blended with such fervor, that, by that love, every individual soul is given a new quality and set in the light of a new meaning; while, at the same time, mankind in the mass receives a great exaltation. We call the love of Jesus a "divine passion" because it had in it, as the word implies, the capacity and the experience of suffering. The love of the greater for the less, of the good for the evil, must have this capacity and experience. Toward man his love was a hunger for souls, "as of space to be filled with planets;" toward God his love was the answer of immeasurable sky, in the deep mirror of the unrippled lake, to immeasurable sky above.

The love of Christ bore within itself the absolute

reasonableness of the divine goodness; and he had the enthusiasm of such a love. That enthusiasm never flagged. It never burst into fierce heats of self-consuming passion. It was a steady, pure flame that no atmosphere of ignorant hate could chill, no gust of temptation extinguish, and no deluge of sorrow quench. It illumined all the way toward love's utmost achievement, and brightened even the seeming defeat on Calvary with the foregleam of an everlasting triumph.

Through all the detail of his ministry we feel the glow of this constant enthusiasm, — in his miracles of healing, his sayings to his disciples and to the multitude, his journeyings and his devotions. Everywhere his love reveals itself and pours its warmth into speech and deed.

But the enthusiasm of Jesus was the product of a divine ideal as well as of a divine passion. At the very beginning of his ministry he uttered a word that has ever increasing significance not only through his earthly life, but also through all the succeeding centuries of his ministry in the spirit to the world. That word was, "the Kingdom." The kingdom of God was the ideal. The prayer which Jesus gave to his disciples, and to humanity, is significant above all in this, that its first petition is, "Thy kingdom come." The revelation of God, the communication of God, and the realization of God in human life, not in the individual alone, but also in society, in the corporate life of mankind, is the end toward which Jesus constantly moved. No such ideal, save in broken, prophetic hints, had ever before shaped itself in the heart of teacher or prophet. Everywhere Jesus carried with him the thought, the spirit, and the purpose of the kingdom, — of humanity redeemed and spiritualized and unfolded into the perfect organic expression of the indwelling divine wisdom, righteousness, and love. He commissioned his disciples to preach " The kingdom of heaven is at hand." His parables cluster about "the kingdom" as their chiefest theme. An earthly crown he refused, but, as the Son of God, he claimed kingship in the realm of the truth.

His idea of the kingdom is more than that of a faint and far ideal. In his mind the kingdom is not something to come, so much as it is the absolute reality that is, and is appearing; and its appearing is the process of the salvation of the world. Jesus' thought of the kingdom of God is the key to the interpretation of history.

Alone in Judea, alone in the world, the Son of God lived and spoke " and wrought with human hands " at the mighty task of the world's salvation; and, through all the centuries since, in proportion to the clearness of their spiritual vision and the depth of their spiritual feeling, men have felt the inspiration of his divine ideal, the powerful attraction of his love, and the quickening glow of his enthusiasm.

But we are not simply studying a character that excites our curious and admiring, perhaps sympathetic, interest. Jesus Christ is come into the world to be the Saviour of men, and, in fulfilling his mission as Saviour, he is their supreme exemplar. He is more than exemplar whom we are to imitate: he is inspirer also, awakening in us motives, as well as setting us a pattern. "To as many as received him, to them gave he power to become sons of God." In fellowship of faith and love with him the nominal sonship of man to God became real and vital. That is the testimony of all deep Christian experience.

We are called to be followers of Jesus, to live according to his spirit and to seek his ends. But to how many this discipleship is a mere formality, — a matter of phrases and ceremonies, — and this service an ill-disguised and loveless drudgery. Many of us, as far as our religious relations and duties are concerned, are in a chill and leaden frame of mind. We are fretted by care, fevered by discontent, and consumed by covetous desire; but no zeal for God has "eaten us up." Whatever we do in the way of out-going religious action is done by a dead lift. We do not move by a strong inward impulsion, the source of which is higher than an uneasy conscience that fitfully wields the scourge. Sometimes, driven by tormenting compunctions and fears, we struggle by sheer force of will into an artificial fervor of speech, and then we utter religious commonplaces in a simulated passion, — words "full of sound and fury, signifying nothing." Sometimes, roused to a sense of shame, and unwilling for the moment any longer to seem what in our heart of hearts we know we are not, we sink into despondency, longing for some force to come upon us from without, and strike or sting us into a condition of sensibility. Any one who can make us feel and weep is welcome.

Thus a transient mood of religiousness is generated, which by and by passes away, leaving our souls more arid and feeble than before.

I describe the condition of some who can always be found in the Church of Christ. Indeed, most of us, at some time, have known this condition in our own experience. What we need, what all who would follow and serve Jesus Christ need, is a vital and inexhaustible enthusiasm. But the objection may be urged that one cannot always be in a state of fervor. The human sensibility will not bear a continuous excitation. The very objection betrays the radical misconception in the mind of him who makes it. Of Jesus it was said, "The zeal of thine house hath consumed me;" and these words described, in its degree at least, not a permanent, but a transient mood. But the mood which they describe was only the momentary intense expression of a continuous capability of feeling, the sudden, transient swelling of a continuous current of emotion. The enthusiasm of Jesus gives us the clew to our need. In his life there were moments of intensified feeling and impassioned utterance; but the continuous main-current of his life flowed on with a calmness and persistence like that of the Gulf Stream in the ocean. Such enthusiasm as his we need; such enthusiasm, in some degree, we all may have; but we can have it only as we have in our hearts the steady and pure warmth of a divine love, and before us the inspiring atttraction of a divine ideal. The love of God as fundamental motive, and the kingdom of God as supreme end, — these, conceived and felt with ever-growing capacity to conceive and feel, will impart to us an enthusiasm in living for God and for humanity that cannot suffer exhaustion or defeat.

There is no true work ever done without enthusiasm. The artist whose heart is cold is a mere artisan. The student of science who works with no great humane enthusiasm for knowledge is only a mechanism more delicately organized than his microscope or his magnetic battery. The statesman who is simply a calculating player with human pawns on the chessboard of a nation or a political party, is less a man than the humblest citizen whom the impulse of patriotism urges to the daily discharge of civic duty, or pushes on to the battle's front in the hour of his country's peril. The deepest secret of life, as well the mightiest force of life, is love. Without love there is no enthusiasm, and without ideals there is no enthusiasm. We freeze our hearts by selfishness and stifle them by sordidness; we fix our eyes upon the little field circumscribed by our day's activities and ends; with no wide-reaching affection and no uplifting ideal, we make of our life a treadmill, and of our duty an unwelcome drudgery; we disclaim the highest endowment of the soul and deny our sonship to God. Narrow faiths and narrow hopes put fetters on the spirit, and small affections keep small the heart and low the temperature of life.

Oh, friends, lift up your hearts to God, that he may make them large with his love. "I will *run* in the way of thy Commandments, when thou shalt enlarge my heart," exclaimed the Hebrew Psalmist. Open your eyes to the meaning and breadth and beauty of God's kingdom, and the glorious vision will stimulate you to high thoughts and noble endeavors, and your hearts will be refreshed with surprising revelations of life's loveliness and worth. Learn to see the individual by your side and the ever widening circle of human souls about you in the light of Christ's enterprise for the world and God's intention toward humanity. Give room for the love of God as motive, and apprehend the kingdom of God as ideal, and no more can the daily task seem trivial, the daily opportunity small, and the daily sorrow vain; no more will your spirit be "cribbed and cabined" by hopeless care; no more will beauty vanish from the earth and glory fade from the sky; no more will you creep and crawl, the companion of grovelling thoughts; but a great sweetness and peace will come into your hearts, and a pure, unwasting enthusiasm will make service a joy and life a triumphal march.

> "What then? A shadowy valley, lone and dim,
> And then a deep and darkly rolling river;
> And then a flood of light, a seraph hymn,
> And God's own smile forever and forever!"

VIII.

CHRISTIAN UNITY.

The ancient barriers disappear :
  Down bow the mountains high ;
The sea-divided shores draw near
  In a world's unity.

One life together we confess,
  One all-indwelling Word,
One holy Call to righteousness
  Within the silence heard :

One Law that guides the shining spheres
  As on through space they roll,
And speaks in flaming characters
  On Sinais of the soul :

One Love, unfathomed, measureless,
  An ever-flowing sea,
That holds within its vast embrace
  Time and eternity.

FREDERICK L. HOSMER.

VIII.

CHRISTIAN UNITY.

That they all may be one; even as thou, Father, art in me, and I in thee, that they also may be in us: that the world may believe that thou didst send me. — JOHN xvii. 21.

THE prayer of Jesus expresses an ideal and prophesies the realization of the ideal. That ideal is a unity of his followers with one another and with God, like the unity of the Son with the Father. It is not a mere agreement, but a fellowship as deep and strong as life. It is an incorporation into a common life, the spirit and impulse and law of which are the love of God.

At the outset there are two things to note. *First:* Jesus, in his prayer, contemplates the whole Christian world. The text is preceded by the the words, "Neither for these only (*i.e.*, the disciples) do I pray, but for them also that believe in me through their word;" and the petition distinctly implies an ultimate universal accession to the faith, — "that the world may believe that thou didst send me." *Second:* the unity for which Jesus prays is the means by which the fulfilment of the prophecy implied in his prayer is to be attained. The oneness of believers in Christ with one another and with God will effect the universal belief in the divine mission of Jesus and the consequent fulfilment of that mission.

There is a splendid daring in the pretensions of primitive Christianity. The early Christians were limited in their out-look by hastily formed and superficial ideas concerning the second coming of Christ; yet they anticipated the triumph of the gospel in all the world. St. Paul, the greatest of all those upon whom was laid the task of promulgating the gospel, again and again confesses his faith in the destined universality of that gospel. This daring the early Church caught from the sayings of Jesus and from the ever-growing significance to them of his life and death and resurrection. In subsequent centuries the Church has not always been true to the first prophetic forecast and confidence. Sometimes overcome by a mephitic worldliness, sometimes depressed by a morbid consciousness of its apparent inadequacy to the mighty task laid upon it, and sometimes possessed by a narrowing selfishness in its interpretation of the divine purpose in creation and in human history, it has deliberately shaped its theology to a limited enterprise and elaborated a dogma of defeat; but always somewhat of the courage and hopefulness of the early faith has survived.

In the first small beginnings of the Church the idea of unity existed rather as a sentiment and experience than as an aim. The early believers were one in faith, in joy, in endeavor, and in hope; but soon differences arose, and these quickly grew into divergences, so that even in St. Paul's time there were embryonic, and even, as in the case of the Judaizers, almost fully developed sects. Yet from the beginning Christians have cherished an ideal of unity, and in various ways, through the ages, they have sought to realize this ideal.

Very early the blunder was made of confounding unity with uniformity. The persecutions of dissenters by the Church that have marked almost the entire Christian history since 325 A. D., though due to various causes, were, in large part, expressions of the persistent desire for unity, and of attempts to secure it. That the Church must be *semper et ubique* — always and everywhere — one was a dominant conviction. The type of unity sought varied, according as the dogmatical, or the sacramental and ritual, or the ecclesiastical and administrative tendency was strongest. As determined by these tendencies, therefore, the unity sought has been (1) dogmatic, or (2) ritual, or (3) ecclesiastical.

The failure to realize completely any one of these types has been notorious. There never has been dogmatic unity; certainly never since the beginning of the fourth century. The Council of Nicæa, the first Ecumenical Council, which was called to secure and preserve dogmatic unity, witnessed the crisis and the new beginning of a strife that divided the Church for several centuries between Arian and Athanasian. Council followed council in rapid succession, and each was more fruitless than its predecessor in the effort to secure the coveted end. For some centuries there was an approach to ritual and ecclesiastical unity; yet even that was not co-extensive with the entire Church, and was more seeming than real. In the religious upheaval of the sixteenth century the Western Church, which had been long separated from the Eastern Church, was rent into fragments even more numerous than the nations that revolted, wholly, like England, or in part, like Germany, from the Church of Rome.

What is the state of the Church to-day, with respect to these types of unity — unity that is confounded with uniformity? There are many different creeds, and different interpretations of the same creed; widely different sects, and different theories of ritual and ecclesiastical order in the same sect. The failure thus far to secure doctrinal, or sacramental, or administrative uniformity in the entire Church has been complete. Christianity has not failed; it has spread wider and penetrated deeper and grown more powerful continually. The elemental gospel of Christ is in the present time as manifestly and as mightily "the power of God unto salvation" as at any time in the past. We may go even farther, and say that essential Christianity has a profounder influence on the heart and mind of humanity than ever it has had.

Now, what is the reason of the failure to which I have referred? The question is exceedingly interesting, and its answer is not difficult to find.

1. In the first place, Dogmatic unity requires universal assent to certain detailed and sharply defined propositions. But men will think individually; they have done so in every other field, and they will do so in the religious field. Thought cannot be coerced. Under certain conditions the expression of thought may be regulated or even suppressed; but the moment the mind begins to act it illustrates that freedom of the will which, however strenuously it may be denied by a school of philosophers, is a dictum of consciousness. Of course thought is never independent of those conditions, existing in heredity, habit, and environment, which shape both the individual and the collective life; but within the sphere of these conditions, in the very nature of the case, thought is unrestrained and unrestrainable. Besides there are certain fundamental laws that inevitably govern the mind's action. Man may be trained or persuaded to a certain uniformity of belief, but the uniformity is always precarious because of the force of individuality in thinking.

Then, too, the world grows. New facts, new points of view, and new ideas, born of increasing knowledge or changing experience, require continual modification of formulas. Such modification is written all over the history of theology. Dogmatic unity could scarcely be secured before it would be broken. Growth is fatal to uniformity. The tendency of progress is toward ever-increasing diversity. That tendency is specially marked in great and critical revolts from established orthodoxy, as, for example, in the Protestant Reformation of the sixteenth century, and in the very real, though unnamed, Reformation, in our own time.

The diversity of theological view which has prevailed with increasing force during the past three hundred and fifty years is charged by Roman Catholic writers to Protestantism; and on this ground Roman Catholic writers have invoked from all religious people the condemnation of Protestantism. But Protestantism is simply a name for a spirit or tendency in the world. The diversity should be charged not to Protestantism but to progress. If Luther had not broken the solidarity of the Roman Church in Europe, some one else would have broken it. The awakening mind that revealed itself in the Revival of Learning and in the new spirit of discovery and enterprise which had its remote spring, in part, in the Crusades, inevitably, sooner or later, must have disrupted the fetters of the defective religious ideas as well as of the defective political and scientific ideas which had so long held Europe in bondage. But is there not, in the intellectual life of men, a tendency toward unity? Yes, but it is unity in simple, elemental principles. As in nature there is a unity of law underlying limitless diversity of manifestation, as in species there is unity of type underlying great variety of feature and function, so in the world of mind there is the unity of fundamental principles of reason and morality as the regulative basis of astonishing diversity of idea and expression. In the realm of religious thought no creed has yet been devised at once simple and comprehensive enough to furnish a perfectly satisfactory basis for dogmatic unity. Not even that noble symbol, "the Apostle's Creed," is adequate.

2. In the second place, Ritual unity requires the universal acceptance of certain definite rites which fully and agreeably express the religious sentiments and adequately meet the æsthetico-religious needs of men. But men have differing needs and susceptibilities and tastes. The same man has different susceptibilities and tastes at different times in his life. Rites appeal differently to different temperaments and different moods. Some people are exceedingly dependent on the expression of religion in forms and ceremonies and mystical emblems; some find these not only not a help but even a hindrance. This is not the place to discuss the question of the authority of rites, but I may observe in passing that the two which unquestionably have their source, as per-

taining to Christianity, in distinct acts and words of Jesus Christ have authority only so far as they are truly ministrant to the spiritual life of men. Even these, Baptism and the Communion, dear and sacred as they may be to us, have no permanent reason of being in themselves, nor even in their original; for the moment they usurp the place of ends in the religious life they become a "snare," like the brazen serpent in Israel. The reason of their perpetuity lies in their real usefulness to the spirit. They have no such position of enduring authority as that which belongs to elemental spiritual truths. Now, in the main, the various divisions of the Church, in their differing estimates and use of rites, at once express and satisfy the religious differences in men. But it is safe to say that there are people in all churches to-day who by sentiment and need belong elsewhere than where they are.

As a matter of fact, the ritual diversities in the Church run all the way from the bare simplicity of the Friends to the elaborate ceremonialism of the High Church Episcopalians or the Roman Catholics. Uniformity in the use of rites does not exist save within comparatively narrow circles.

3. In the third place, Ecclesiastical unity demands adherence to a certain fixed organization and administrative order. But the churches exhibit nearly as wide differences in polity as they do in creed or ceremonial, and the differences are due to

much the same causes as those which render dogmatic conceptions and ritual observances various. The element of individuality is as powerful, as irresistible, in the practical as it is in the theoretical realm. Differences of ecclesiastical order and administration are due, in part, to the same causes as those which make civil order and administration various. Political tendencies and forms undoubtedly affect ecclesiastical ideas and methods. For example, democracy is unfavorable to a hierarchy; at least, it is far less favorable than absolute monarchy. Roman Catholicism has been consistent with its fundamental idea in supporting a monarchical form of government. Roman Catholicism in America, instead of being an exception, proves the rule. It has been confessedly strong, and, until recently, reactionary, partly because of its historic genius, and partly because it has been recruited continually from countries in which men are trained in its fundamental ideas of authority and administration. Yet in America it is changing, slowly but surely moving toward democracy. It feels the stimulus of freedom and the moulding force of the eager life about it; and inevitably, if slowly, is modifying its peculiarities. The Roman Church is one thing in Spain; it is quite another thing here in America. Congregationalism is the creation of men bred with the instincts and passions of liberty. It is strongest where political liberty is greatest, as in England and America. Congregationalism comprehends, of course, not only other bodies than that one technically designated Congregationlist, as for example, the Unitarian and Baptist denominations, but also bodies in which the Congregational principle has great influence.

Now, Ecclesiastical unity requires universal assent to a certain type of Ecclesiastical organization. But where is the type? The absolutely comprehensive type does not exist. Not all men will become Roman Catholics, though many men cannot as yet be anything else. Not all will become Episcopalians, nor Congregationalists or Baptists, nor Methodists or Presbyterians. Each of the polities represented in these various denominations, or groups of denominations, has enormous defects. Few thoughtful men are perfectly satisfied with the church of which they are members. This is not due to mere discontent with their peculiar situation or relations. It simply shows that the ideal is larger and other than the real.

All sects and denominations are in the nature of the case transient; they express conditions and moods and present necessities of the great social mind and heart. They may last long; they doubtless will last long; but the longer they last the greater will be the modifications through which they will pass. What will those modifications be? They will be modifications of such peculiarities as are extreme and divisive; not merely of those that simply appeal to different tastes, but of those that separate and excite revolt. Churches will modify toward each other.

As no sociologist has yet given us the type of society to which we shall attain in our social progress, — though types have been fashioned with great skill and insight, from Plato's Republic to Bellamy's Co-operative Commonwealth, — so no ecclesiologist has shown, and no denomination exhibits, the type of a Universal Church; while all denominations have elements and features that will belong to the Church of the future and of humanity.

So far our study has been descriptive and critical, and perhaps oppressively negative. Let us turn to the positive side. What, then, is the unity for which we may rationally hope? What is the unity toward which, under the leadership of Christ, we are surely moving? I venture no prophecy as to organization. Organization will conform to spirit and life.

The unity to which the whole Christian Church must come, is (1) the Unity of Obedience to the law of love.

"Show me a church," said Abraham Lincoln, "whose creed is love and I will join it." The Church that shall endure must be one whose law is love, — love to God and love to man. That law has its supreme exemplification in Jesus Christ. He is the head of the body, not only by historic divine ordination, but also by inherent spiritual fitness. The rallying point of the whole Christian world to-day is not a creed, nor an ordinance, nor an ecclesiastical principle, but Jesus Christ; not dogmatic conceptions of him, nor dogmatic formulas about him and his plan of salvation, — as to these men differ and will differ, — but the living, loving, mighty personality. The unity in him is not devotion to a school, but love to his divine-human self, with all that he expresses of revelation from God in terms of human life and character, and loyalty to his spirit of truth and righteousness and love.

The unity to which the whole Christian Church must come is (2) the Unity of Devotion to Christ's aim: the salvation of men from ignorance and despair and sin, the ennobling of life by the disclosure of its divine possibilities, and the realization in the world of the Kingdom of God.

On this broad basis all men who love God can unite. By this powerful attraction all are drawn together. Selfishness, whether of the individual or of the society, divides; love unites. The enterprise of pure and self-sacrificing benevolence draws into its current all streams of moral activity. The perpetuation and extension of a sect or denomination is not a true end, save instrumentally. We seek to develop a strong denomination, as we seek to develop a strong family, for the service of the community, the nation, and the race. But in the family-idea there is a permanency which is not in the denomination-idea. Our great aim as Christians is not to transform men into so many more Episcopalians, or Unitarians, or Baptists, or Methodists, or Congregationalists; but into so many more Christians — so many more men and women and children who know and love God, and are ruled by the spirit that is in Christ; so much more of Christ's redemptive work done through his body which is the Church Universal; so much more of the realized Kingdom of God.

The law of love and the enterprise of love strike deeper than all forms of dogma or ritual or ecclesiastical organization. The appeal of these is to the deepest that is in the heart and soul of humanity.

What will result from pre-eminently seeking this unity? There will result, *First:* the recognition of similarity beneath diversity. Among lovers of Christ and God and humankind differences of creed and ritual and polity will grow like differences in feature and accent and dress, giving picturesqueness, perhaps, to life, but raising no bar to sympathy and fellowship. There will result, *Second:* the permanent change of emphasis from the incidental and the inferential to the essential, leaving free play for diversity in thought and method. There will result *Third:* the establishment of such relations between different churches and denominations as will consolidate their energy and economize their force in the great and absorbing work of spiritualizing men and Christianizing society and the world. The present economic wastefulness of the Church, through excessive individualism and consequent disunity, is lamentable if not criminal. There will result *Fourth:* the development of a vast moral and spiritual power over society. The Church has vast power even now, but its power is little compared with what it might be. How much of beneficent force is now unutilized and incapable of being utilized by the Church! How much of culture — not dilettante culture, but real, solid culture — is now separated from the Church and unsympathetic with it! The remedy for this is to be found in a fuller spiritual life expressed and operant in a more vital unity. The early Christians were victorious because of that spirit which made observers exclaim: "How these Christians love one another!" If we are one in love and unselfish service for all men; if we are one as Christ is one with the Father; we shall move upon the consciousness and heart of the world with an undreamed-of power.

Still more, the unity of the Church in obedience to the law of love, and in devotion to the aim of Christ, must have the subjective result of deepening and purifying the inner life of the Church, of clarifying its thought of God, and of developing a theology that shall be as profound and as comprehensive as its love. Unity in love precedes and produces, not follows, unity in thought. "He that desires to do the will of God" — that is love reaching forth into action — " shall know of the doctrine." We must live more soundly in order to think more truly. Love leads us into the head of Christ and of God, and from the heart of God we read the deep secret of His eternal purpose.

But what shall we say of such strong movements toward Church unity as are indicated by the " Lambeth Articles," issued by the Protestant Episcopal Church of the United States and the Church of England, and the propositions of the National Council of the Congregational Churches of the United States? We must hail them with thankfulness and revived courage. They show that the spirit of Christ, which is in his people, is striving toward fuller and more harmonious expression in the organic life and activities of the entire Church. It is too early to predict, with any confidence, the result of these movements; but it is not too bold to affirm that they are signs of a new consciousness developing in Christendom, and to believe that they point to a unity of the Church, in the near future, closer, more vital and more beneficently influential on the life of the world than any that has been attained in the past.

While welcoming these tokens of a better day, we must turn our minds afresh to the primal spring of all true life and all true thought, and to the creative principle and energy of a radical and enduring unity. The influence of Jesus Christ draws all who discern his spirit into the unity of love for God and man, and that unity finds ever richer expression in the great engagements of Christian worship and work.

Slowly but surely the dawn of a new day brightens our sky. With rejoicing we behold the unmistakable signs of the time, — signs that, through all the strife over Scriptures and creeds, and even by means of this strife, God is leading mankind to a deeper life of the soul in him and a clearer understanding and a larger appropriation of the spirit and purpose of Christ.

Beneath all the multifarious diversity of ideas in the Church, there is already a common life of thought, sympathy, mutual understanding, and mutual impulse toward the one great end for which the Church exists. There is a powerful movement in human society toward real religion. There is a drawing together of hearts and minds toward the divine centre of life. There is a vast unuttered prayer in the very throes and strivings of modern society which, as it grows articulate, voices itself in the words, "Thy kingdom come. Thy will be done, as in heaven so on earth." God speed the day when all men shall say with deepening faith and love: "I belong to the Church Universal, — the body of Christ, the Family of God." Let us hasten the coming of that day by yielding ever more complete obedience to the divine law of love and by increasing devotion to the one great unifying aim of the Lord Jesus Christ. Amen.

IX.

THE CHURCH, THE BODY OF CHRIST.

One holy Church of God appears
    Through every age and race,
Unwasted by the lapse of years,
    Unchanged by changing place.

From oldest time, on farthest shores,
    Beneath the pine or palm,
One Unseen Presence she adores,
    With silence, or with psalm.

Her priests are all God's faithful sons,
    To serve the world raised up;
The pure in heart, her baptized ones;
    Love, her communion cup.

The truth is her prophetic gift,
    The soul her sacred page;
And feet on mercy's errand swift,
    Do make her pilgrimage.

O living Church, thine errand speed,
    Fulfil thy task sublime;
With bread of life earth's hunger feed;
    Redeem the evil time.

                    SAMUEL LONGFELLOW.

IX.

THE CHURCH, THE BODY OF CHRIST.

Now ye are the body of Christ. — 1 COR. xii. 27.

SUCH is the significant figure by which St. Paul represents the Christian Church. He conceives the Church not as a formal institution or structure, and certainly not as a mere aggregation of believers, but as a living organism of which Christ is at once the head and the animating soul. His fundamental idea of the individual Christian life, as consisting in union with Christ, appears in his idea of the Church.

Jesus used the vine as a figure of his relation to his disciples: they were branches unified in himself, the vine, and vitalized by the life which he supplied. The two figures have an essential similarity. The element of vital unity is fundamental in both. In the one figure, the branches are knit into the vine; they draw their life from the vine; they cannot exist, certainly cannot be fruitful, apart from the vine. In the other figure the members cohere in one body, share a common life, and fulfil their various functions under the directive impulse of one head. The figure of the apostle, used for a purpose somewhat different from that of the Master, is more specifically a concrete representation of the Church as an organic agent in the world.

Jesus did not write a book nor create an institution; he imparted a life which naturally and spontaneously became organic in the Church. Individual Christians have functions as various as their capabilities and opportunities, but they all cohere in one body that has one head and is animated by one life. This primary truth does not conflict with the administrative independence of the local church, but it is easy to see that the doctrine of independence pressed too far divides Christ. The Church is representative of Christ in just so far as, in the exercise of its proper functions as the body of Christ, it embodies his spirit, manifests his life, and fulfils his mission. It perpetuates the personal touch of the Lord who once moved among men, the concrete expression of divine wisdom and holiness and love. Its life is an immediate, continuous gift. Its authority is derived not through a long succession of priestly consecrations, but through immediate communion — a continuous interior contact — with Christ.

There is immense value in historic continuity, but the real authority of the Church does not repose in that. The Church lives because Christ lives; his life in it is the essential condition of its perpetuity. Ordinances, offices, and creeds are incidents; the life of Christ is essence.

What makes a church — an apostle? But churches were founded in Antioch and Rome, and doubtless in other places, without the presence or even knowledge of an apostle. Does a bishop constitute a church? A bishop is but the creature and functionary of the Church. Is it a Declaration of Faith, a meeting-house, a set of officers and a periodical service that constitute a church? No; it is Christ, the informing life and law of a body of people who are doing Christ's work and living out his principles in the world. The presence of the divine Spirit is the only essential constituting force and the only absolutely valid consecration.

Now, then, if the Church is the body of Christ, what is its function? What is it to do? What is it for? This question is asked to-day, in a hundred practical ways, with an insistence never so strong before. It must be answered, and the only answer that can successfully endure the trial to which it is subjected by human experience and needs, as well as the searching criticism of awakened and penetrating intelligence, is the Church's visible embodiment of Christ's thought and spirit, and its demonstrable fulfilment of Christ's purpose among men. Christ as the head of the body rules and directs the Church. Christ as the innermost spring of the Church's life determines its character and its work.

Let us look at the figure and the truth which it presents to our minds more closely. The body is the instrument of the informing soul. It expresses the temper and executes the behests of the soul. When the soul is gone the body is dead; under the influence of certain stimulants or irritants it may simulate life, but it is dead.

The figure, like all figures of spiritual fact or truth, is inadequate; it is suggestive, but not exhaustive. The human body has no independent will; it cannot revolt against or utterly disregard the dictates of the mind, though through lack of discipline it may hinder the mind; of itself it has no volitional power. The Church as a body may revolt against or disregard the will of Christ, as well as, through lack of discipline, imperfectly execute or even impede his will. But when it thus revolts against Christ it ceases any longer to be the body of Christ. Being the body it is instrumental, it is subject to the soul.

The Church as the body of Christ exists: —

(1) To express the *spirit* of Christ toward God and toward men.

(2) To utter the *message* of Christ from God to men.

(3) To do the *work* of Christ — to carry on the divine reparative and redemptive activity within and upon the hearts, minds, bodies, and estates of men.

1. In the first place, then, *the Church is to ex-*

press the Spirit of Christ. It is to express the spirit of Christ toward the Father: the spirit of reverence and worship toward the Infinite Goodness and Holiness; the spirit of trust through every experience whether of sorrow or joy; the spirit of obedience to every command, and of submissiveness under every trial; the spirit of happy confidence in God, of filial communion, of thankfulness and praise.

As the features and hands of Jesus, as his whole form was obedient to his feeling and thought, — now bowed in prayer, now uplifted in adoration, — so the Church is to express in its attitude toward God the indwelling spirit of Christ. If the Church is irreverent, wanting the true impulse of worship, so that its prayer and praise are not natural and sincere; if it is distrustful and indocile; if it is indifferent or resistant to the influences of the Holy Spirit, is it not misrepresenting Christ? What is the motive that impels us to practise religious observances? Is it not often mere habit, or an uneasy sense of duty? Our responsiveness to the spirit of Christ is the only certain sign that Christ is "formed within us."

The Church is to express also the spirit of Christ toward man. It is his face to show his smile of kindliness, or his look of tender love, or his frown of holy indignation against impudent wrong. It is his eyes to weep tears of pity over human sorrow, his lips to breathe words of comfort and compassion, his ears to hear the complaints of the stricken, his heart to bear the burdens of the oppressed. It is to express in its manner the gentleness and meekness of Christ, his charity toward the fallen, his sympathy with all who suffer, his patience with all who are ignorant and wayward. The fallen and the outcast are to find in its look the compassion and gracious welcome of Christ. "The woman that was a sinner" is to hear from its lips mercy and not judgment. Little children are to find its arms outstretched to receive them. Whatever is evil and harsh is to have no place in its speech or manner. It has nothing to do with pride or arrogance; nothing to do with cold neglect or cruel scorn. To it must not belong enmity or envy or selfishness in any form. In so far as it shows any of these traits or tempers it belies its informing soul; it betrays Christ when it perverts in expression the spirit which is proper to him. Think of the frightful and colossal misrepresentation of Christ of which that church is guilty, in which there is contention, or coldness, or worldliness, or uncharitableness, or pride, or envy, or greed for possession and place and power, or irreverence, or indifference to human need, or forgetfulness of human sorrow, or unforgivingness to offenders, or devotion to luxury and selfish ease!

I wonder if we think of this as much as we should. The apostle exhorts the Christians to whom he writes to "put on Christ," that is to show fairly the Christ who by their profession is in them. We think much of what Christ is to us as a Saviour from the penalty of sin, and somewhat of what he is to us as Lord commanding us to service, but what are we to Christ? How are we expressing him? What sort of translation of his speech are we making to the world? We are members of the body of Christ, not simply for our own safety and comfort, but for his use as the means of his continuous self-manifestation to humanity. The world is to see Christ in us, if it is to see him at all.

2. In the second place, the Church, as the body of Christ, that is, his instrument and means of expression, *is to utter his message* — the message of God through the Christ to the world. It is his voice, putting into articulate speech his thoughts — his conception of the infinite and eternal Father, his word of truth for the enlightenment and comfort and salvation of men. As the organ of Christ, the Church must express truly, not personal opinion, not predilections and prejudices determined by association, habit and inheritance, and not mere dogmas, but the very mind of Christ. To preach the gospel is not merely to repeat what has been said in the past. The living Christ in his living body freshly utters his living message to the minds and hearts of men. That message is not a mere reminiscence or record of something past, but a

testimony of the present love and mercy of God, the present grace of salvation, the present power of the cross, the present inspiration of the Holy Ghost, and the present experience of the resurrection and the eternal life. Only as Christ lives in us are we fit or able really to give his message. All our preachings and publishings, our professings and testifyings, are meaningless and powerless unless the indwelling Christ speak in us and through us. The word which is "in demonstration of the Spirit and of power" is "the word that was in the beginning with God," and is henceforth and forever incarnate in human personality.

The consciousness of this truth is what gives the Church power when it speaks. It does not put itself in the place of Christ, substituting a tradition or an institution for the living personality, but freely yields itself to Christ that he may have ever fresh utterance through it as his living body.

3. In the third place, the Church as the body of Christ *is to do the work of Christ*, — to carry on the divine redemptive and reparative activity within and upon the hearts, minds, bodies, and estates of men.

This is the point upon which I would lay special emphasis to-day, for it needs emphasis. The Church, with some clearness, has recognized its mission and obligation to utter the message of Christ. Of this every missionary organization is a witness. To some degree the Church has recognized its duty to express the spirit of Christ in its life. But it has not yet, at all fully, recognized its function as the executor of Christ's will in carrying on his work. The larger part of the Church's endeavor has been to convince men of the truth of the Gospel, — to make them hear and persuade them to believe the Christian message, — to convert individual men from unbelief to faith, and from sin to righteousness; and in doing this work it has often been more anxious to commend its own claims and authority than purely to propagate truth. But, for the most part, it has stopped there. Like a recruiting officer it has sought to enlist men, company after company and regiment after regiment, but it has not in any large sense led them to battle. It has not attacked the intrenched evils of vice and poverty and ignorance and selfishness with any such breadth of plan and practicalness of method as it should, as, indeed, it must attain if it is even fitly to express the indwelling Christ, to say nothing of possessing the world for him.

I am not unmindful of the vast and multifarious charities of the Church in all ages since its beginning; nor would I in the least depreciate the very great moral influence of the Church, even in the darkest hours of its long experience; but what I would do is sharply to call your minds to the defectiveness both of the method of the Church and of the idea of its mission which has prevailed in it through most of its history. That defectiveness grows more apparent as society develops and new needs clamor for ministry. Recall the story of Christ's actual life among men as that story is told in the Gospels. What a strenuous life, and how full of action it was! Jesus talked much; the records, full as they are of his speech, give us but fragments; but he labored more. Take the Gospel of Mark: from beginning to end it witnesses to a steady march of activity. Mark's Gospel is the biography of the toiling Christ. In it we see the Master incessantly engaged in works of mercy, — healing the sick, feeding the hungry, comforting the sad, refreshing the weary, and teaching the ignorant.

Is it not significant that Jesus was so busy in daily, practical philanthropy? He seems to have laid fully as much stress on works of mercy as he did on words of truth. In his reply to John's inquiry: "Art thou the Coming One?" he bade the Baptist's messengers "go and tell John what things ye have seen and heard." The Messiah's credentials are quite as much in his works as in his words; and in his works not as miracles merely, but as manifestations of divine pity and benevolence. His exhortations to his disciples are continually on this line — of engagement in the works which are characteristic of the gospel of good-will. One of his great promises is, "He that believeth in me the works that I do shall he do also; and greater works than these shall he do." He was speaking, not of thaumaturgic display, but of blessed achievements in ministry to human need. When he sent forth the seventy on an evangelizing tour he gave them power to heal the sick and cast out demons; and his charge was, "Freely ye have received, freely give." They were not merely to preach a gospel; they were not merely to promise men a heaven by and by. They were to preach a gospel, broader and sweeter than men had dared to hope for; but they were also to attack directly the palpable evils of human sickness and pain and hunger and blindness and poverty and crime.

Now the Church, as the body of Christ, is certainly commissioned to do the works of Christ. *That is what it is for.* "The word" and "the works" are not to be separated. "The word" needs the illustration and enforcement of "the works." And yet, even we who live in this enlightened time have recollections of a temper in the Church that was suspicious of philanthropy. Philanthropic enterprises were looked at askance, almost as if they were devices of Satan to beguile men from the security of faith into the deadly peril of trust in works. Under the influence of a mistaken conception of faith the Church, especially the Protestant Church, narrowed its work until the Christian spirit which is broader than any church sought and found instruments for its purpose outside of all ecclesiastical organizations. Why has a multitude of agencies — societies, guilds, associations, salvation armies, — sprung up to do philanthropic work? Because, for a time, the Church failed to recognize that it is itself, in the design of Christ, the great philanthropic society of the world. How narrow the sphere of the Church still is in the thought of many people! It must not meddle with politics, though cities fester with political corruption. It must not engage in " secular " matters. Its work, it is said, is "spiritual," and the word, "spiritual," has been dessicated and bleached until it is a poor thin ghost of religiosity, having no practical meaning.

No; if Christ healed the sick, the Church may, and must, heal the sick. If Christ cast out demons, the Church must cast out the demons of vice and greed and crime-breeding want. If Christ fed the hungry, the Church must feed the hungry of body and mind and soul. The great question for the Church to grapple with to-day is a question not as to the revision of its creeds, but as to the revision of its life. There is need that the best thought be engaged in the endeavor to correct the mistaken and still too prevalent idea of the Church on this matter of its relation to the actual life of men and society to-day, and in the endeavor to adjust the machinery and force of the Church to the work which as the body of Christ it must do, or itself become a corpse, offensive to men and inviting burial.

The Church must no longer stand apart from the

great currents of human activity and the great spheres of daily human interest. It must no longer dwell in a cloister or a prayer meeting. It must strip for action. It must gird itself and bend to wash weary disciples' feet. It must have training schools, and orphans' homes, and hospitals, and medical dispensaries, and classes for the study of economics in the light of the New Testament, and reading-rooms, and play-rooms, and all means for making life healthy and pure and skilful and strong and joyous. The recent dedication of a gymnasium in a Christian school[1] in the city of Springfield, as the first of its prospective buildings, is full of inspiring significance. The Church must have all these and many more facilities and instruments for its work. It needs the prayer-meeting and the services for worship and meditation. To these it must come to get head of power, then it must turn the power on in such ways and through such agencies that society shall be moved and changed and shaped into the visible and growing kingdom of God. It must widen its material ministry that its spiritual ministry may be wider and more efficacious.

But there are still some, perhaps, who will ask: Will not this secularize the Church? Did it secularize Christ to go into the streets and into the homes of men — to pour out his power in ministries of health to the paralytic and the blind? Did it secularize him to furnish wine for a wedding-feast

[1] The Y. M. C. A. Training School.

and bread for a hungry multitude? No; it will not secularize the Church to pour out its energies in daily ministries to ignorant, unskilful, needy, and suffering humanity; but it will spiritualize the home, and consecrate business, and sanctify social life; and it will react on the Church to make it more like Christ than it ever has been. The body of the Lord should be strong and beautiful and rich with manifold skill. This is the mandate of God to the Church to-day to " make its calling and election sure." Heeding this mandate the Church will grow in that beneficent power which it was meant to possess and wield amidst the life of the world. It will draw men to it as by a celestial gravitation; and its divine message, reinforced by its divine works, will grow clearer, sweeter, more eloquent, and more convincing. Its voice will no longer be, what too often it is now, like a solitary cry from the house-top — a mere Muezzin-voice calling to prayer the throngs that do not heed. It will no more be a rival institution unsuccessfully competing with humanitarian organizations and lecture-bureaus, alternately jealous of the State and fawning upon it for unrighteous favors; but it will be "the light of the world," guiding men in all industries and studies and recreations, and leading them in the pathway of faith and love and holiness, making its promise of heaven in the life that is to come potent with the working of a heavenly spirit in the life that now is. It will be "the salt of the earth," cleansing its foulness, staying its corruption, and healing its disease. It will be the poor man's friend, the weak man's support, the oppressed man's helper, the rich man's monitor and the strong man's guide. It will be the savior of society, dispelling strife from its industries and fraud from its commerce, subduing its greed for gold, purifying its politics, banishing its misery, developing its virtues, and multiplying its joys. Not less clearly and strongly, but more clearly and strongly, it will preach its saving gospel of a crucified and risen Lord and Redeemer of men; and it will make the world, what God means it shall be, the perfected kingdom of his glorious Son.

X.
THE INCREASE FROM GOD.

WE feel Him, nor by painful reason know!
The everlasting minute of creation
Is felt there; Now it is, as it was Then;
All changes at His instantaneous will,
Not by the operation of a law
Whose maker is elsewhere at other work!
His hand is still engaged upon His world —
Man's praise can forward it, Man's prayers suspend;
For is not God all-mighty? — to recast
The world, erase old things and make them new,
What costs it Him?

Is not God now i' the world His power first made?
Is not His love at issue still with sin,
Visibly when a wrong is done on earth?
Love, wrong, and pain, what see I else around?
       ROBERT BROWNING.

X.

THE INCREASE FROM GOD.

I planted, Apollos watered, but God gave the increase. — 1 COR. iii. 6.

THE Church in Corinth was full of factions. Instead of thinking of Christ, and following Christ, and doing Christ's work for men, these Corinthian Christians were looking to Christ's servants who in various ways or at various times had been their leaders. The spirit of partisanship was rife. Some said: "We follow Paul." Others said: "We follow Apollos." Still others said: "We take Peter for our leader." The result was that the Church was not only divided and weakened in its force for good, but it had become even obstructive of true Christian endeavor. Both the efficiency and the charm of the Church were well-nigh lost. Paul's words are full of reproof as well as of instruction. He tells those Corinthians that they are carnal and not spiritual. The spirit which they show is not the spirit of a truly Christian Church. Their force, instead of being directed faithfully and persistently to the ends which Christ is seeking through them, is turned into a self-divisive and self-destructive energy. They have violated their allegiance. Who is Paul? Who is Apollos? Who is Cephas? These men are but ministers, that is, servants, of Jesus Christ. Christ, not this or that apostle, is the head of the Church. To Christ the Church owes undivided loyalty; in Christ alone it finds its true unity as well as its ground of being.

What a picture that Corinthian Church presents! How many times since Paul's day has the Church presented a similiar spectacle, — partisanship spoiling unity, jealousy outraging love, and contention destroying spirituality. Is there any sight more shocking and revolting than a church of Christ in which love has grown cold, and selfishness has soured the milk of human kindness into the acid of rancorous hate, and religious life has ebbed away leaving only a repulsive simulacrum of doctrinal "orthodoxy"?

But we will not dwell on the offensive picture. With reproof the apostle mingles instruction. That instruction is pertinent to the condition and needs of the Church to-day, if the rebuke is not.

The function of the Church, in large outline, is to do the works of Christ and to publish the message of Christ. This involves a work of internal conservation and development — of training and unfolding itself in all Christian knowledge and grace and efficiency. Its great mission to men, as the depositary of the Gospel, demands all its resources of thought, feeling, possessions, and skill in labor. Upon the Church is laid the work of saving the world through the gospel of Christ. Now, even if the Church were never invaded by factiousness, nor fettered by ignorance, nor weighted down by sloth, still how greatly disproportionate to its resources and strength is the work that it is set to do; that is, when we look at the Church alone. But we are taught by Jesus Christ, we are taught by the Apostle Paul, and we are taught by experience, not to look at the Church alone. The work of saving humanity and bringing it on toward its high spiritual destiny is God's work. He is not limited by our organizations, nor dependent on our resources. Many times the Church falls to looking to its organization, or to some one of its specially capable servants, as the chief means, if not the only means, for establishing the divine kingdom in the world. In the Corinthian Church some said: Paul is the great man; everything depends on him. Others said: No; Apollos is more eloquent; he is the essential power. Others pinned their faith and their partisan devotion to some one else. With words that smite like cords, Paul declares the truth that must confound and shame the shallow-minded sectaries. "What then is Apollos? and what is Paul? Ministers — servants — through whom ye believed; and each as the Lord gave to him. I planted, Apollos watered; but God gave the increase. So then neither is he that planteth anything, neither he that watereth; but God that giveth the increase."

Here, then, is the truth that the Church must ever remember, that Christians need to ponder upon until its meaning has got into their hearts and suffused all their thinking and inspired and energized all their action:

1. All true power is of God.

This is true in the realm of the natural life. That was a profound saying of St. Paul's, beyond which none of our philosophies have got: "In Him we live and move and have our being." Everywhere are the divine life and the divine energy. The world is the effluence of God's thought and the objectification of his will. The globe thrills with vitality because he pervades all things. The springing green of the meadow, the purpling clusters of the vineyard, the waving gold of the harvest, and all the multiform fruitage of field and forest are the product of the divine energy. We live and walk and think, the blood leaps in our arteries and our nerves tingle with sensation, because God is. All life is a divine product and manifestation. The true doctrine of Creation is a statement of the divine immanence as well as of the divine activity. All human endeavor has its sphere within and not outside of the sphere where God works, for he works everywhere.

All result of man's labor is a divine product. The farmer tills his fields and sows the seed; but

God in the sunshine and the rain and the fecund earth gives the harvest. Nothing, not even the commonest task, is done apart from Him.

> "The hand that rounded Peter's dome,
> And groined the aisles of Christian Rome
> Wrought in a sad sincerity;
> Himself from God he could not free."

The poet, with eyes that see, helps us to see the inseparableness of God from the lofty achievements of genius; but the hand that rounds an axe-helve, or shapes the keel of a ship, is also dependent on that Deity from whom no man can free himself in time or eternity.

We fancy that God made the world and set it to run its course under the regulation of laws which he has impressed on it; but there is a subtle infidelity in our fancy. He is in the world, the life of its life, the energy of its action, and the force of its development. A true insight into nature gives us

> "A sense sublime
> Of something far more deeply interfused,
> Whose dwelling is the light of setting suns,
> And the round ocean, and the living air,
> And the blue sky, and the mind of man:
> A motion and a spirit, that impels
> All thinking things, all objects of all thought,
> And rolls through all things."

The higher the plane of being and activity the more manifest to thoughtful minds is the all-pervading presence and energy of God. Whence come the great thoughts of genius? Whence come our true thoughts, that dawn like stars out of the infinite dark? As God is the begetting force that enriches the earth with a new creation every springtime, and flings abroad its million-fold products in grass and flowers and bourgeoning trees, so God is the underlying and genetic force of all our true thinking. He makes the fair products of the human mind as certainly as he makes the autumnal harvests. He is in all things and he accomplishes all real results. By him the world subsists, and in him man lives and moves and has his being.

When we rise to the spiritual plane the causal relation of the divine life to the human, as the ground and spring of all spiritual perception, feeling and will, becomes even more apparent. Jesus said to his disciples: "Without me," that is, apart from me, "ye can do nothing." He identified himself with God because he was the Son of God, and his words are declarative of our necessary relation to the divine life. If apart from God we can be nothing, surely apart from God we can do nothing.

The world is in ignorance, animalism, and sin. The greatest fact of all human experience is salvation. It is the deliverance of man into the full and free life of the spirit. To us is committed a message of grace which is "the power of God unto salvation." What shall we do? Manifestly we must faithfully and purely and unceasingly declare this message. Can we make men believe the message? Can we penetrate to the dormant spirit, close-folded in the flesh, and waken it to life and action? Can we unseal the fountains of spiritual aspiration and feeling, and set free their healing streams? In our best ministry to the world we are but instruments; we are but more or less serviceable conductors. The life is from God. He who "turneth the hearts of kings, as the rivulets of water are turned" by the gardener when he irrigates his field, turns every heart that ever is turned to himself.

The doctrine of efficacious grace so tenaciously held by the old Calvinists has in it a core of vital truth. They were wrong in the narrowness of their theory of grace, and in their presumptuous attempt to prescribe the methods and limit the scope of the divine activity. But in this they were right: it is God who begets man into the life of the spirit. Back of all our instruments and organizations, our exhortations and preachings, our pleadings and prayers, is the irresistible divine attraction. God in Christ, God the Spirit of all grace and truth, God the Father and Sovereign of men, is the Saviour of men.

We look at our schemes and enterprises and array of organizations, and talk about what we have done for God; meantime it is God who has done all for the world and for us. Without this ever-present, ever-prevailing, divine activity, the scope of which we have no power to measure, all our plans and machinery and endeavor would be but lumber and noise. We look upon the slow march of humanity up out of dark ignorance, and enslaving superstition, and brutal vice, and we say: This that we have devised has done it — the eloquence of the preacher, the strength of the argument, the perfectness of the machinery; and, while praising God in words, praise the instruments in our thought. But God is the real worker. Over all our agencies and enterprises is the brooding, ever-working Spirit, whose ways often are not our ways, and whose work sweeps a circuit the breadth of which we have not dreamed.

Here is the truth which the apostle presses upon the Corinthian Church: "It is God who gives the increase." Paul may plant wisely and widely; Apollos may water carefully and often; but in God only are "the promise and potency" of abounding harvests.

2. The clear recognition of this truth and hearty, trustful acceptance of it, are the essential conditions of power in the Church to accomplish its work of saving men by bringing them into the life and joy of the kingdom of God. So essential are the recognition and acceptance of this truth, that failing here, whatever may be our seeming success through many and curious devices, we utterly fail

of accomplishing our true work. God will not fail. Men will be saved. The Redemption of the world through Christ is the declared purpose of the Almighty. But we shall fail, and miss our own blessed share in the great enterprise. Our dependence must not be on any material or artificial means. Sometimes Christian men have thought, or have seemed to think, that the work of a church could be fully accomplished by securing a fine location and a beautiful building and exquisite music and eloquent or scholarly preaching; and in this delusion they have supplied these conditions and then folded their arms in complacent expectancy. To such the stern voice of experience declares, that, unless the false idea and the fatuous hope are abandoned they will perish in disappointment, if not, at last, in self contempt.

The power that makes a radiant, far-shining splendor on the top of yonder lamp-post is not in the crystal globe that surrounds the carbon pencils, nor in the carbons, nor in the insulated wires, nor in the whirring dynamo, nor in the panting engine; back of all these correlated pieces of mechanism is the cosmic force which streams forth in the sunshine, the force by which ages ago the sunbeams were locked up in the forming coal-strata, until at last they are set free in our streets to make plain the path of the belated traveller. The power that makes luminiferous and effective the Church of Christ is not its elaborate and nicely articulated machinery of pastor and officers and committees and meetings, but the divine Spirit who works in all and through all to accomplish divine ends.

But does this truth in any slightest degree obviate the need of instruments and organizations and individual and united labor? Must not Paul still plant, and Apollos still water? The figure suggested by the apostle is singularly fit. It is God who gives the harvest, — God in nature, God in the soil, and the rain, and the sunshine, and the shade; but the farmer must plough and sow and watch and weed; he must guard the tender growth, and, when the harvest hour strikes, put in the sickle and reap. This is man's share in the complete divine process. And God works in the farmer too, giving him life and prudence and skill of mind to interpret and use nature. By his faith in nature, that is, in God, the farmer works. Because a force above him makes sure the harvest, he sows in hope and reaps in gladness of heart. I say the apostle's figure is most fit. So must we, in the realm of the spirit, cultivate and plant and guard and reap. So shall we do if there be in us true faith in God.

For the truth that we have been contemplating is (1) a source of inspiration to endeavor. The greatness of our work, looked at, as we so often look at it, from a low plane, would paralyze us with discouragement. Think for a moment, if you can, of a man who, having no knowledge of nature's processes and no faith in the reproductive relation of seed to soil and sun and shower, is told to produce twenty bushels of wheat from the one bushel that is set before him. What marvel could be greater to him than that which he is asked to perform?

When we get some true idea of what it is to save men from sin, we at once see how futile is our endeavor unless we believe in the ever present and ever efficient grace and power of God. But, having a true and strong faith, we overlook all difficulties. The hardness of the task disappears. It is God's work; we are but instruments, servants of a divine purpose. With faith comes a great inspiration. We know that God is not mocked. "Whatsoever a man soweth, that shall he also reap." The farmer springs to his work with joy, knowing that the earth waits but to respond to his toil with rich reward of golden harvests. So we, if our hearts are filled with the great thought of God's power and purpose to redeem the world, spring to our work with joyful and patient assurance, knowing that "his word shall not return unto him void."

(2) There is great comfort, too, in this truth. When the days are dark and the obstructions are mountainous, then the resources of the soul in God more deeply disclose themselves. Experience lets us into the meaning of St. Paul's words: "When I

am weak, then am I strong;" "I can do all things through him who strengtheneth me." The conviction that we are engaged in a divine enterprise gives us the heart to work on when work seems fruitless. God's work will be done. The harvest is his, and in his time he will produce it in all its fulness and all its beauty. No toil for his ends is vain. No seeding is lost. No right effort utterly fails.

(3) There is power in this truth. Confidence makes man invincible. The confidence which a profound belief in God imparts is the most unconquerable thing in this world. If you believe that God is the Lover and Saviour of men, and you have any true conception of him, defeat to-day is no token to you of defeat to-morrow; failure to-day contains no omen of failure at last. Defeat cannot be final. Failure cannot continue. The nature of God alone is an inviolable guarantee of the triumph of good and the salvation of the world. The deep sense of God as the absolutely efficient force in the redemption of man perpetually feeds in our hearts the springs of motive as well as of hope. We are workers together with God; nay, it is God who, of his own good pleasure, works in us both to will and to do.

Instead, then, of a true faith making our endeavor seem unnecessary, it stimulates us to greater endeavor and lifts us to a higher power of sustained effort to enlighten and move and save our fellow-men. The divine method and activity include all our instruments, all our organizations, and all our aspirations and prayers and efforts. God makes our planting and our watering vital parts of his great enterprise. In the productive processes of nature, as in the germination and growth of plants, every zephyr and rain-drop and sunbeam and starbeam has its place of efficient relation to the full result. So in the realm of the spirit, the multifold ministries of God to man through man, — the words that we may speak, the deeds that we may do, the prayers that we may breathe, the influences that we may wield, — all have an efficient relation to the great end which, after all, is wholly divine.

The truth that "God giveth the increase," whosoever may do the planting and watering, instead of being an excuse for our sloth and unfaithfulness, is a supreme reason why we should pour our energies without stint into the work of bringing men into the knowledge of truth and into the life of the spirit. It is a great stimulus to endeavor. It is a great inspiration to sacrifice for the end in view. It is a measureless reinforcement of power to live and to work along the line of God's redemptive purpose. A wise bishop once said: "I tell my clergy to believe as if God did everything and nothing depended on them, and to work as if everything depended on them." We must do our work or God will give us no increase. He will save the world, but not by us. Our service measures our capacity to receive divine grace and joy. It is at once the fruit of our faith and the attestation of our faith. Intelligent consecration, wise diligence, and sweet spirited zeal in doing good to our fellow-men and bringing them to a knowledge of their Saviour, Jesus Christ, with all that this beautiful service involves, are the only fit acknowledgment we can make of God's boundless goodness to us and of our grateful trust in him. It is only the "living sacrifice" that is a "reasonable service," and this is a service of unwearying faith and unconquerable hope.

> "The veil of Time a moment falls
> From off the Eternal's face:
> Recede the old horizon walls
> To give fresh breathing-space:
> And all who lift their eyes may learn
> It is our Father's will,
> This world to him shall freely turn
> A world of freedom still."

XI.

FORSAKING ALL FOR CHRIST.

Religion 's all or nothing: it 's no mere smile
O' contentment, sigh of aspiration, sir —
No quality o' the finelier-tempered clay
Like its whiteness or its lightness; rather stuff
O' the very stuff, life of life and self of self.
                              Robert Browning.

XI.

FORSAKING ALL FOR CHRIST.

Whosoever he be of you that forsaketh not all that he hath, he cannot be my disciple. — LUKE xiv. 33.

WHAT did Jesus mean by this saying? We who have avowed ourselves, or secretly consider ourselves, Christians are in the habit of calling him Teacher and Lord. It is a fair question whether even we have clearly recognized and radically accepted a tithe of all that is involved in the supreme Teachership and Lordship which, in words at least, we so promptly ascribe to him. It is a startling experience, — to be brought suddenly face to face with some of Christ's sayings. I wonder how many of us are willing to pull ourselves up with a strong hand and compel our minds to consider honestly and unflinchingly the words of our Teacher until we see exactly what he taught and what his teaching involves with respect, not only to our habitual conduct, but also to our ruling motives and dispositions and purposes.

The world is busy in getting and using for purposes of multiform gratification the things to which its needs or its tastes give value, and we are part of the world. Whatever may have been the dominant idea of the Christian in the past, to-day and here the average Christian is both in the world and of the world. That is, the solidarity of society is stronger than the theological division of men into "saints" and "sinners." If love of art, devotion to politics, interest in inventions, and eager pursuit of economic prosperity are marks of "worldliness," then the church is worldly, and external differences between Christian and non-Christian, or rather, between church member and non-church member, are often hard to find.

That there are differences, very wide and deep, between the really Christian man and the really un-Christian man, there can be no doubt; but the superficial marks of difference between the nominally Christian and the nominally un-Christian man often are not discernible to the ordinary eye. Christians are no longer a "peculiar people."

This fact I cannot now consider at length; though I must say that, if clearly understood, it is not necessarily an evidence of retrogression. No one who understands the real character and tendencies of modern society will hazard the opinion that it is degenerating, that social conditions are less favorable to virtue now than they were in the past, or that essential Christianity has lost anything of its virility and force. But I mention the fact in order to call your attention sharply to this thought: that we who are avowed disciples of

Jesus Christ are bound, now as never before, to know just what Jesus Christ teaches, and now as never before are bound to look our own life squarely in the face under the light of what Jesus Christ teaches. The consciousness that we are in the world, and, in a very large sense *of* the world, gives a fresh poignancy to such sayings of Jesus as this: "Whosoever he be of you that forsaketh not all that he hath, he cannot be my disciple."

Before we take up the study of these words in their relation to our daily life, let us pause for a moment to consider two preliminary thoughts. (1) The first is the importance of construing particular sayings of Jesus in the light of his entire teaching. Many moral precepts, like many statements of truth, are conditional. Each is, to some extent, dependent on other precepts. Take, for example, the commandment which has a primary place in Christian teaching: "Thou shalt love the Lord thy God with all thy heart, and with all thy soul, and with all thy mind." This must be interpreted by those revelations of God which disclose his essential lovableness. No command could compel or justify love of a moral monster. It is the exhibition of the divine nature which Jesus gives us that makes the command so authoritative. The command is not simply an edict: it is an appeal to what is highest in us, because God is set forth in his Son as the One absolutely good. The command, "Thou shalt love thy neighbor as thyself," also must be interpreted by those revelations of the ideal human nature which Jesus makes, and which give us the standard of a true self-love, and therefore the standard of a true love for our neighbor.

If, now, these simplest, most elementary statements of moral duty need the interpretative light of other statements, much more do many of Jesus' sayings need the interpretative light that shines in the general drift and purport of his whole teaching. Take this, for example: "Except ye eat the flesh of the Son of man and drink his blood, ye have not life in yourselves. He that eateth my flesh and drinketh my blood hath eternal life," in which is expressed, if we take these words literally, the rankest religious materialism. But we remember that Jesus said: "The words that I have spoken unto you are spirit, and are life." Therefore we must go beneath the surface and behind the form and beyond the letter, or we shall not only fail to understand the real meaning of our teacher, but we shall even get a contradictory and false, or wholly absurd, meaning. If we do not use a large good sense in our study of Jesus' words, we must make him sometimes an impracticable enthusiast, sometimes a mystical ascetic, and sometimes a radical and destructive revolutionist.

(2) In the second place, we must read the sayings of Jesus in the light of this truth: that the im-

mediate, continuous, and imperative reference of these sayings is to life. They are not subjects for curious speculation, nor appeals to blind credulity. They enounce principles of righteousness and generate pure motives; they quicken the reason, sensitize the conscience, stir the feelings, and rouse and guide the will by the power of truth. Through Jesus' words we feel the vital and vivifying breath of the Holy Spirit; by them we are instantly urged on from moral perception to moral action; they bear immediately on all our doing; they are directly related to our daily purposes, dispositions, and deeds, and attain their final results in our characters. In every saying there is some suggestion of duty as well as some pulse of inspiration.

The strange doctrine is still sometimes advanced that Jesus did not give the Sermon on the Mount as a law of daily conduct, but rather as the expression of an unattainable ideal, the function of which is to drive men to despair, and thus make them willing to trust Jesus to do everything for them in their stead. Such a doctrine makes Jesus a trickster with words, and takes the heart of sincerity out of the revelation which is mediated by him. It is not only an erroneous doctrine: it is even an immoral doctrine; and it lies very close to the root of the worst errors in dogmatic theology. The sayings of Jesus are designed to shape human conduct and character. They appeal to faith, but it is a faith " that works by love " and conforms to fundamental principles of reason and morality. The conclusion of the Sermon on the Mount is tremendously suggestive of what must be the outcome of Christ's teaching: "Every one therefore who heareth these words of mine, and doeth them, shall be likened unto a wise man, who built his house upon the rock. . . . And every one that heareth these words of mine, and doeth them not, shall be likened unto a foolish man, who built his house upon the sand."

But while we have no right to push the teaching of Jesus aside as impracticable, and seek refuge in the soft indolence of a trust which is soporific to conscience and stultifying to reason; on the other hand we are not to lower his teaching to the level of our habit or of an easy attainability. We must understand his sayings in their harmony with his own perfect personality. Weakness, cowardliness, and selfishness in us make some of his teachings impracticable. But while in his heart there is infinite patience with men, in his doctrine there is no lowering the standard of excellence toward which we are to aspire and strive; there is no dropping the ideal to the level of our little thought and low attainment. Listen to his words, — words that smite like whips, that pierce like arrows, that shock like electricity, — "Why call ye me Lord, Lord, and do not the things which I say?"

How greatly important it is, then, that we find

out just what Jesus did say, and just what are his instructions to us and his requirements of us in this day! Too often we treat his words as a charm or a fetish, instead of what they were meant to be, — a light for our feet and a lamp for our paths.

Take, now, this saying: "Whosoever he be of you that forsaketh not all that he hath, he cannot be my disciple." The word translated "forsake" is rendered in the American revision by "renounce," and means, literally, "to separate one's self from." If we follow Count Tolstoï's method of interpretation and understand this saying in a badly literal way, then we must admit that there is very little real discipleship even among those who profess to follow Jesus. We must admit, too, that most of us are either profoundly mistaken in our conceptions of the Christian life, or utterly recreant. We have no right to qualify the text simply to save ourselves. But let us see whether Jesus does not himself both qualify and explain this "hard saying" in such a way as to reveal at once its deep spirituality of thought and its entire, though not easy, practicability.

We will approach the text first negatively. From what we know of Jesus' teaching as a whole we are sure that here he does not mean, (1) That it is the duty of every man who would follow him to abandon all material possessions. Situations are conceivable in which it would be one's supreme duty to surrender utterly, not only possessions, but even life itself, for the sake of Christ, or that for which Christ stands. But in general this manifestly is not a duty. To abandon all hold upon material possessions, and therefore all use of them, would be to put one's self out of relation to the economic and social prosperity of men. It would be to rupture important social ties, and to shear one's self of a great part of his power to serve his fellowmen. The real service of man is the true service of God. The field of service is not confined to what we call our spiritual relations. At every point where life touches life, whatever the interest may be, — economic, political, social, or religious, — there is the opportunity for service; there love may have free play; there we may worship by unselfish and wise deeds the divinity revealed in man. Whatever is done to promote the real good of men, though it be building a factory, or laying a railroad, or opening a mine, or improving the sanitary condition of a crowded city ward, or founding an industrial school, or endowing a library, or any other of the numerous beneficent enterprises that require money and labor and economic skill, is as much a part of service to God as praying and singing hymns and planting missions. Christianity sanctifies wealth to the highest and widest uses. It sanctifies also the righteous production of wealth. But the production of wealth implies society and co-operation and the thousand-fold relations and activities of industrial life. Jesus does not mean, then, that simple abandonment of all material possessions is a necessary condition of discipleship to him.

A wide and careful study of Jesus' teaching makes it plain also that the text does not mean (2) That we should sever all ties of home and society, and abandon kinsfolk and friends as well as possessions. For to do this would be to repudiate or evade the broadest and weightiest obligations which Jesus himself declared and emphasized. The hermit or the celibate is not the true type of the Christian. God hath set the solitary in families. The family, not the individual, is the unit of society, and society is the sphere of the individual's true development. No man liveth to himself alone. No man can live to himself alone and remain in the true sense a man. Humanity is not an aggregation, but an organism. We are necessary to each other. Religion, as Christ reveals and exemplifies it, does not isolate, it consolidates, men. It makes a true society possible. Love is the ultimate, supreme, divine law of the world. But love implies relation, communion, mutual action and mutual service. Any view of Christianity which draws us apart from our neighbors is a false view. The Pharisee excluded the common people; Jesus haunted the streets and homes where thronged and dwelt the "publicans and sinners." A true perception and acceptance of Christ's spirit strengthens and ennobles all human relations. The apocalyptic figure of heaven is a great city, whose length and breadth and height are equal, — the symbol of completeness. The city is the highest type and expression of social organization. The isolation of savagery disappears as the spirit of Christian civilization appears, and Ishmaelites become brothers and co-workers. Society is our field, our opportunity, the fulfilment of our own life, the embodiment as well as the revelation of the kingdom of God.

Just what, then, did Jesus mean when he said, "Whosoever he be of you that forsaketh not all that he hath, he cannot be my disciple"? When he spoke these words he was addressing the multitude. The Evangelist says: "Now there went with him great multitudes; and he turned, and said unto them, If any man cometh unto me, and hateth not his own father, and mother, and wife, and children, and brethren, and sisters, yea, and his own life also, he cannot be my disciple. Whosoever doth not bear his own cross, and come after me, cannot be my disciple." Then follows the brief parable about the necessity of counting the cost. To this parable the text is in the form of a logical summing up and conclusion: "So therefore whosoever he be of you that renounceth not all that he hath, he cannot be my disciple." Surely these are strong words, and they sound strangely enough on the lips of a man who is seeking followers. There is truth in the remark of a recent writer on those seemingly terrible words: "If any man cometh unto me and hateth not his own father, and mother, and wife, and children, and brethren, and sisters, yea, and his own life also, he cannot be my disciple." " A slow beast needs sharp goads, and Christ stirs and startles the conscience by such awakening words, not as giving laws of action, but spurs to reflection." There is truth, I say, in this, but not the whole truth. Jesus uses words that startle and sting, but his paradoxes are not self-contradictions. The multitudes ran after him with a feverish curiosity, and a fickle enthusiasm awakened in great part by selfish desire. It seemed an easy thing to be disciples of this Nazarene prophet. Perhaps much would be gained by following him. Poverty and sickness and sharp discontent might be relieved. At any rate, here was a new interest, a new possibility, and the inviting intoxication of a new enthusiasm. But Jesus, patient as he is and divinely compassionate, will not let the poor fools of their own fancies be deceived into a course which they have not fibre and force to maintain. He will not let down the ideal of human life which he comes to disclose. He will not accept less than the complete redemption of men, though he must wait long for it. In effect, he tells the people: " You know not what you seek. You are eager to gain something on the low plain of sordid and selfish life. Listen: he who would come after me must renounce all things, even himself, and take a cross."

Does he not touch here, with sure hand, the

secret malady of all human life? Men seek that they may have; Christ would have them seek that they may become. "A man's life consists not in the abundance of the things which he possesses." Life is participation in the thoughts, feelings, purposes, possessions, and achievements of the Spirit. We are prone to estimate all things, and even to look on all relations, from the selfish point of view. What Jesus seeks is not to take away possessions, or dear objects of our love, but by a change of spirit and motive in us to set us in a new and true relation to all possessions and all objects of affection. It is the same doctrine which he urges in the words: "Seek ye first," that is, as chief, "the kingdom of God, and his righteousness; and all these things shall be added unto you." It is the doctrine of that self-surrender which issues in one's finding his true self: it is losing the soul to save it.

Here appears the deep reason of Jesus' method in putting himself as God's representative, as God's Son and man's Saviour, first. This is why he says: "Believe in me," "Follow me," "He that loveth father or mother more than me is not worthy of me." He puts himself first because he would have God first in the human soul. Man finds his own fulfilment and salvation in the love and life of God. The change from the Ptolemaic, or geocentric, to the Copernican, or heliocentric, system of astronomy is vividly illustrative of what Jesus would do for us. As Copernicus put the sun instead of the earth in the centre of the planetary system, so Jesus would put God instead of self in the centre of the moral system. The selfish spirit of the world, and of our own hearts, reverses the true order of life. Our common phrases are tell-tale. We ask concerning a man, "How much is he worth?" meaning, How much of material wealth has he? There are no material measures for the worth of the soul; not merely because the soul of man may survive the wreck of the material cosmos and enter upon a destiny of endless bliss or endless woe, but because the soul is the man, the child of God, the participant in essential life. Selfishness is the bondage and prison of the soul: it creates for us false standards, and begets in us mistaken estimates of values. Selfishness emphasizes having at the expense of being. The thing usurps the place of the spirit.

The "forsaking all things" which Jesus demands is just that surrender of the selfish instinct and the selfish point of view which every one makes, and must make, and makes gladly, wondering that he had not made it long ago, who opens his heart to the Son of God as Saviour and Lord, and Inspirer and Guide. To such a one possession becomes stewardship. Things have for him value only as they become instruments of love in its glad, multiform ministry to the world. The surrender of the selfish point of view changes everything. It transforms life. It takes no worth from arts and industries, from railroads and mills, from commerce and currencies. It gives all these a new value. The man has changed, and so they — the things which have all their worth by their relation to man — are also changed. Forsaking all that he hath, in the surrender of his heart and will to God, he ceases to follow things, and becomes a follower of God manifest in his Son. Jesus' words strike a blow at the instinctive and unconscious idolatry of the human heart. The words are strange to us: we cannot understand them, because we have not sought first the kingdom of God, or have done this as yet only in a groping, tentative way.

What Jesus asks of us is something utterly radical. No half measures will satisfy him or truly serve us. "No man can serve two MASTERS." "Ye cannot serve God *and* mammon." In our sin and selfishness we are ruled by what we possess. We are the slaves of the material. In the life of the spirit which Jesus opens to us, it is as if everything fell away from us. Nothing has value save as it is new-found in the love and thought of God. A new sense of value comes to us then. Wealth is precious as the instrument of the spirit in attaining worthy ends. All human relationships are sweeter, tenderer, and more sacred. God, having become first in our lives, with himself gives us all things anew, and then the forsaking, the renouncing, that seemed so hard, reveals itself as the open doorway for our entrance into the measureless liberty of the heavenly life.

Self-renunciation has been called "the secret of Jesus." It is an open secret for those who will hear his voice and open their hearts to the life of God in him.

What Jesus asks of us, then, is not the mere abandonment of all material possessions, nor the severing of domestic and social ties; but the abandonment of that selfishness in possession and that self-love in our affections which perpetually hinder us from apprehending the true value of those and the sacred dearness of these. What he seeks is that abandonment of ourselves to God which makes it possible for God to give himself to us. It is that coming to him by faith which is salvation, and the appropriation in time of the life which is eternal.

> "O wealth of life beyond all bound!
> Eternity each moment given!
> What plummet may the present sound?
> Who promises a *future* heaven?
> Or glad, or grieved,
> Oppressed, relieved,
> In blackest night, or brightest day,
> Still pours the flood
> Of golden good,
> And more than heartful fills me aye.
>
> "My wealth is common; I possess
> No petty province, but the whole;
> What's mine alone is mine far less
> Than treasure shared by every soul.

Talk not of store,
Millions or more,—
Of values which the purse may hold,—
But this divine!
I own the mine
Whose grains outweigh a planet's gold.

"'All mine is thine,' the sky-soul saith;
'The wealth I am, must thou become;
Richer and richer, breath by breath,—
Immortal gain, immortal room!'
And since all His
Mine also is,
Life's gift outruns my fancies far,
And drowns the dream
In larger stream,
As morning drinks the morning star."

XII.

A QUESTION OF THE HEART.

THE people listened, with short, indrawn breath,
And eyes that were too steady set for tears,
This one man's speech rolled off great loads of fears
From every heart, as sunlight scattereth
The clouds; hard doubts, which had been born of death,
Shone out as rain-drops shine when rainbow clears
The air. "O teacher," then I said, "thy years,
Are they not joy? Each word that issueth
From out thy lips, doth it return to bless
Thy own heart many fold?"
      With weariness
Of tone he answered, and almost with scorn,
"I am, of all, most lone in loneliness;
I starve with hunger treading out the corn;
I die of travail while their souls are born."

HELEN HUNT JACKSON.

XII.

A QUESTION OF THE HEART.

Now when Jesus came into the parts of Cæsarea Philippi, he asked his disciples, saying, Who do men say that the Son of man is? And they said, Some say John the Baptist; some, Elijah; and others, Jeremiah, or one of the prophets. He saith unto them, But whom say ye that I am? — MATT. xvi. 13-15.

WHY did Jesus ask this question? It is a perfectly natural question for a man to ask, however great he may be. If, for a few minutes, we can rid our minds of the prejudgments which hide from us the real, susceptible, human nature of Jesus, we shall, in part at least, and in a perfectly true way as far as it goes, understand why he asked this question.

No man in the world is entirely sufficient unto himself; he was not meant to be so. He was made for fellowship and sympathy. That is neither a natural nor a true idea of life which makes one absolutely independent of his fellows, either by lifting him above them or sinking him below them. Our related life is as elemental and as necessary to complete being as our individual life. Our related life is indeed the sphere of morality; for right and wrong have no meaning save in the contacts of man with men. It is the sphere of our virtues and our affections. To love and to be loved are possible only through our relation to other like beings. Even the affection of man for brutes is based upon a certain rudimentary likeness and kinship. Love for God is possible only as God is in personal relation to us through some real likeness.

Certain rare experiences for a time isolate men from their kind. The thinker who thinks far draws apart from less strenuous minds around him, and in his deepest thought he finds fellowship among only the few. Genius is essentially lonely. It is all, however, a question of degree. The tie of man to men is never broken. This partial isolation of soul is not pleasurable, even when it is slight; when it is great it becomes a Gethsemane. Only a deep sense of divine communion can sustain one who by profound spiritual insight and much holiness is lifted above the world of common men and women. As he draws nearer to God, his love for men and his sympathy with them grow greater indeed; but at the same time the power of men to understand him and sympathize with him is lessened. Only when they rise to his level can there be entire responsiveness and communion between them and him.

But in the common life that we know, and of which our lives are part, we feel the need of our fellows, — the need of sympathy and appreciation.

We like to be understood. It is not a mere liking: it is a necessity of our nature, if we are to be happy. This sense of kinship and community of life is not merely an essential to comfort; our lives fulfil themselves in and through our fellow-men. Our love is greatened by its reflex in the love of others for us. Our thought attains full breadth and reality only when it comes back to us in the thought of others. Emerson, speaking of the quickening power of sympathetic appreciation on our minds, said: " I can say to you what I cannot first say to myself. Other men are lenses through which we read our own minds." Our best thoughts are not born of solitude, though they may come into consciousness in solitude. They are the reflex of our mind's activity on other minds. Often in conversation with intellectual and sympathetic people we surprise ourselves by our capacity to think and utter wise or witty sayings. So also our affections unfold themselves in the stimulating environment of loving hearts. Our virtues are often elicited, confirmed, and enlarged by sympathetic and virtuous companionship. In the company of heroes the craven soul becomes almost heroic. Generosity becomes almost easy to the covetous man when generous souls surround him.

We need appreciation. We need the reassuring touch of a true sympathy. That sort of faith in ourselves which is essential to true courage often is dependent on the faith of others in us. In every sphere of life men lean much on their fellows, and draw much from them. Particularly in the higher spheres, such as those of teaching and preaching, in whatever manner these functions may be fulfilled, do men need and long for the support of human sympathy and responsiveness. Often he who has most courage, and most strength to stand alone, has the deepest craving for appreciation. This craving is the mark of a noble nature. He who seems, and as far as the world is concerned is, most fully sufficient unto himself is least willing to be sufficient unto himself, and suffers most from isolation and from the coldness, misinterpretation, and opposition of those about him. The perception of this truth, which comes through experience, makes possible such utterance of it as we find in Helen Hunt's poem, "The Teacher."

To many of us, the higher and finer sorrows of the unappreciated spirit may not be intelligible: to the vast majority of men they certainly are not intelligible; but every one has some capacity for suffering from want of sympathy and appreciation. How the heart sinks at the thought, which some incident — some experience of coldness, some rebuff of affection by rude indifference — has forced upon the mind! "I am not understood. Those to whom I look do not sympathize with me. My motives are misconceived. My real self is not appreciated." More often than otherwise the thought does not shape itself into words: it is scarcely so much thought as feeling.

Much of the pain and bitterness of life have their spring just here, — in the incapacity or unwillingness of our fellows to see just what we are and what we are aiming at, and in their unresponsiveness to our purpose or our mood. Here, in the family circle, is a child or youth whose nature, touched to finer issues perhaps than that of the others, suffers almost daily from the unconscious cruelty of paternal inappreciation or fraternal indifference. Here is a wife whose soul has capacities for love and service that are never recognized, or whose mind is eager with desire for knowledge and tremulous with the aspiration to mingle with the deeper currents of human thought, but who must live on year after year, growing daily more deeply conscious that the best that is in her is unseen and unprized. Here is a husband in whose heart is a whole store of strengths on which there is no draft, or whose finest thought and tenderest feeling ever recoil upon himself from the hard surface of an insensible nature by his own fireside. Here is a teacher whose best resources are unperceived, and who drudges at the task of instructing dull minds in commonplace facts, when he might soar and shine, and enlighten and inspire, were there any appreciation of his real power and any response to its appeal. Here is a preacher who has passed on from the rude elements of religion in ordinance and dogma to the inspired perception of the highest and broadest truths of the spirit, but who is "cabin'd, cribb'd, and confined" by the dulness, bigotry, and impenetrable sordidness of the "religious" men around him who have no capacity to understand him and power only to oppress his heart and hinder his free utterance. The prophet cries out of an anguished soul: "Who hath believed our report?"

There is, perhaps, no feature of life more tragical than this, — the littleness of appreciation which the finest spirits must meet. Real sympathy with the men and women that are nearest to us, true understanding of their hearts and minds, and just appreciation of the best that they can think and feel and do, are of slow growth in this world. Prophets and benefactors are prized after they are dead, and monuments of stone or brass express the tardy recognition of worth that contemporaries could not see, or understand.

It is the glory of the faithful souls in every walk of life that they did their work though it was not prized; that they spoke their word though, when it was uttered, it was unheard or was scorned; that they loved though they were loved not, and died of hunger; that they fought the fight, though no victor's laurel gladdened their longing eyes as they grew dim with death.

Was Jesus in any way dependent on the appreciation and sympathy of men? We cannot doubt it. As surely as he was human did his human heart long for human recognition, human appreciation, and human responsiveness. It is in the nature of the good and sincere man to wish to be known and appreciated. This wish is not caused wholly by perception of the truth that one must, in some measure, be known and appreciated in order to be effective in accomplishing the full benefit that he is seeking to work out for men. It is certain that all highest spiritual blessing is a personal communication. "This is the eternal life," said Jesus, "that they know thee, the only true God, and Jesus Christ whom thou didst send." To know and appreciate God is the ever inviting and ever uplifting goal of the spiritual mind. That men might know God, Jesus came and taught and lived and died. That men may know God, they must know him whom God hath sent. "No one knoweth the Son, save the Father; neither doth any know the Father, save the Son, and he to whomsoever the Son willeth to reveal him."

Jesus' power to bless men was limited by their power of recognizing and appreciating him. Only as they rose to a true perception of his character and spirit and purpose could they become plastic to him, to be moulded by him into his own image. His very success as Saviour depended on his ultimately winning the love and faith and obedience of human souls; therefore it was vital to his mission that men should know who he, the Son of man was. This is apparent throughout the Gospels. It appears in the preaching of the apostles recorded in the Acts. It is scarcely less clear in the Epistles of St. Paul and St. John. Genuine Christianity has won its way in the world, not through the promulgation of dogma and the enforcement of ritual, but through man's growing spiritual appreciation of Christ. The personal apprehension, the personal relation, the personal response, the personal devotion, and the personal assimilation to the mind and character of Christ, — this is the real triumph of the Gospel and the salvation of men.

Undoubtedly Jesus' perception of this truth, that the success of his mission lay in winning men truly to know and appreciate him as the Son of God, was clear, and undoubtedly it underlay the question to his disciples: "Who do men say that the Son of man is?"

But this was not all. The wish, the longing, for sympathy and appreciation was not caused simply by his perception of the truth that he must be known and loved in order to be effective in accomplishing his purpose. The human heart in him longed for human recognition, human love, and human appreciation of his motive and thought and endeavor.

We cannot carefully and sympathetically read the life of Jesus without feeling this again and again. Recall a striking incident recorded by St.

John in his Gospel. Jesus had set forth the spiritual nature of his mission and of discipleship to him in plainer and more searching speech than ever before. He had set forth the dependence of his disciples upon him in a figure so startling, even to the Oriental mind, that his hearers revolted. "Except ye eat the flesh of the Son of man, and drink his blood, ye have not life in yourselves." The explanatory words, "It is the spirit that maketh alive; the flesh profiteth nothing," rather confirmed than lessened the revolt. Those sense-loving and self-seeking men who listened to him and who had even begun to follow him, outwardly at least, were dismayed and offended. They said: "This is a hard saying; who can hear it?" And from that time many of his disciples went back. They were not equal to the test. They would follow him for the "loaves and fishes," or even while there was hope of loaves and fishes; but they could not renounce themselves and take up the cross; they had no deep and true sympathy with his nature or aim, and they could not rise with him to that realm of spiritual thought and feeling and endeavor where he always dwelt. What pathos, what sad and wistful yearning, there is in the Master's voice, as he turns to the chosen twelve with the inquiry, "Will ye also go away?"

Those of you who are intimately acquainted with the New Testament will recall other incidents which show Jesus' instinctive demand for sympathy and true appreciation. Why did he take Peter, James, and John with him on the Mount of Transfiguration? Was it that he might give them a dramatic display, a sort of pedagogical representation, of his real, though invisible glory? No, no. With all his desire and purpose to instruct and inspire, and to qualify them by exceptional revelation for their exceptional work, he longed to have them know him more fully, and, in some deeper measure than ever before, to enter into the real meaning of his life and work. In Gethsemane also he took with him these three disciples. Poor and disappointing companions they proved; but their dulness and inability to comprehend him only serve as a foil to bring out more clearly the yearning of this vast spirit for fellowship and sympathy in the very crisis of his passion and pain. The heart of Jesus was reaching after sympathy and appreciation in this question: "Who do men say that the Son of man is?" and still more in the direct appeal to his disciples: "Whom do ye say that I am?" There was much more than this in these questions, but this certainly was there. When Peter's reply came with prompt and earnest confession: "Thou art the Christ, the Son of the living God," there was a thrill of deep joy and exultation in Jesus' answer to the confession: "Blessed art thou, Simon, Son of Jona, for flesh and blood hath not revealed it unto thee, but my Father who is in heaven."

This was a moment of pure, human joy to Jesus, notwithstanding that, a few hours later, Peter's inspiration was quenched by the ignorant egotism which impelled him to rebuke the Master for prophesying his own approaching violent death. There were such moments in the life of Jesus. Lonely as he was in the greatness and elevation of his nature, lonely as he must be by the very character of his mission in the world, here and there he found responsive and sympathetic souls; here and there he found those in whom his spirit awoke a true appreciation and love. It is reasonable, as well as pleasant, to think that the home in Bethany was one of the places where Jesus found a love that was unselfish and an appreciation that approximated the purity and loftiness of his own spirit.

But, for the most part, his work was done alone. He was not understood or he was misunderstood. Men did not deeply know him, nor did they prize him for what in him was highest and noblest. "He came unto his own, and his own received him not." Few out of all the multitudes that thronged him in the city streets or by the lake-side had any true perception of his nature and mission. He trod the wine-press alone. Moved to wonder and admiration by his works of healing, some said: "This is the Messiah." Solemnized and quickened in conscience by his teachings, some said doubtingly: "He is a prophet." Some gave him the name of Elijah, or Jeremiah; and others identified him with the still remembered ascetic, John the Baptizer. "Even his brethren did not believe on him," and the disciples who were nearest to him and lived in daily intercourse with him did not know him till after he had drunk the cup of human suffering to the dregs and had passed beyond their sight.

What all this experience of loneliness in the midst of men, this want of sympathy and appreciation from kindred spirits, meant to Jesus it is difficult to tell. It is an aspect of the Christ-life that we have not contemplated, or have not understood. That he was "a man of sorrows and acquainted with grief" we dimly see, but we have had little true perception of the reality and range and depth of his sorrow. He was an alien in the midst of his own kin, made alien by the very greatness of his love, and the very fulness and elevation and purity of his nature. We wonder not that his earthly life was short. Jesus died a young man. Yet measured by its experiences, his life was long. From Bethlehem to Calvary was a far journey.

But the main thing to note now, if we have come to any clear and true idea of Jesus' life, on the side of its want of human sympathy and appreciation, is, that through all he endured. No want of appreciation weakened his purpose; no lack of love for him lessened his love for men; no unreceptiveness checked his giving; no misinterpretation diverted him from his aim; no coldness chilled his passion for the salvation of humanity. The pledge of the conquest of the world was in his calm, assured patience. He knew himself, if men did not know him; and he knew that the Father knew him. Once he said: "I am not alone, for the Father who sent me is with me."

Lonely as he once was in the midst of the world, he will not be lonely when again his shining feet press the walks of men. He is less lonely now as he moves invisibly among the people, still present though unseen, working in hearts his slow but sure work of grace, and saving the world by the vivifying power of his spirit in human life. Not known, not appreciated, not loved once, be sure he will be known, appreciated, loved and worshipped at last by all. To him every knee shall bow, and every tongue shall confess with thanksgiving that he is Lord. Peter's answer was prophetic. At last all the world will say: "Thou art the Christ, the Son of the living God."

The appreciation of Jesus to which men will come, to which they are slowly coming, will be as many-sided as his nature. At one time his followers have emphasized, and even caricatured, the sacrificial aspect of his life. At another they have emphasized his power over nature and evil spirits. At still another, they have seemed to appreciate, with some breadth and fulness, his divine character, as revelatory of God. But all our views have been limited. All our appreciations have been partial. We have looked upon him as a divine functionary, pre-eminent in a specific relation to men; but we have not grasped, and known, and felt, and loved his whole personality. But he can wait to be known, sure of man's entire heart and mind at last. And we shall know him as he is when we rise to his level, when we are like him.

An apostolic writer tells us that "for the joy that was set before him, Jesus endured the cross, despising the shame." Was not that forecasted joy, in part, the realization of the fulness of his own life in the life of a redeemed humanity? It must be so.

As we contemplate this aspect of Jesus' experience, which the incident related in the text brings vividly before us; as we see Jesus subject to that kind of suffering, compared with which ordinary pains and trials are insignificant; as we see him, the very incarnation of love and sympathy, and loftiest thought and finest feeling, and purest virtue and freest self-sacrifice, living his life amidst coldness and sordidness and suspiciousness and inappreciation, deepening sometimes into fierce enmity; as we see him loving men with a divine love, and pitying them with a divine pity, and reading their hearts with a divine insight, and knowing himself at the same time to be an alien in the world, unrecognized, save by here and there a rare soul; — as we see him thus, at once the most human and the most divine of all men, made solitary by eminence in suffering as well as eminence in worth, with a heart as wide as the world, with a capacity and desire for love and sympathy and appreciation as great as his capacity for loving and serving and understanding, yet living, toiling, and dying without the consciousness of being understood, prized, loved, and sympathized with in any great way by a single human soul; as we see him, despite this, steadily fulfilling his mission, flinching from no trial, avoiding no burden, never faltering in his difficult path, setting his face steadfastly towards the great end for which the Father had sent him into the world, and bearing his mighty load until his heart broke on the cross, — what a revelation comes to us of his greatness! What a manifestation of God in humanity shines upon us! What a flood of meaning is poured upon our life! What lessons of faith and consecration and patience are pressed upon our minds! And what disclosures are made to us of our own littleness, and weakness, and selfishness! What humiliation we feel, remembering our complainings under trial, our faithlessness in hours of temptations, and our unheroic and craven spirit when men have withheld from us their sympathy, or have met our efforts to serve them with resistance or contempt.

As we contemplate the Son of man, let us learn some lessons that will lift our lives a little nearer to his.

We, too, must often suffer from want of genuine

human love. Often we are misunderstood by those who are nearest to us, our best qualities are overlooked, our noblest endeavors win little appreciation, and our purest motives are misinterpreted. Many a day we must toil with no reward of grateful recognition. The more finely we live, the purer our taste, the loftier our thoughts, and the more unselfish our deeds, the more surely much of the life about us will be inappreciative and unsympathetic. What then? Jesus walked alone though his heart hungered for companionship. We can be faithful. We can hold fast to the best. We can resist the temptation to let ourselves sink down to lower level. Every soul that rises toward God must mount by a cross of suffering; but he lifts the world toward God. We shall not be utterly alone. Though men know us not, the Father will know us. Though our path be lonely, Jesus passed that way before us, and walks it with us again. It is good to love, though we are not loved. It is good to serve, though our best service is not prized. It is good to attain heights of knowledge and spiritual vision, though we pass beyond the sympathetic recognition of our fellowmen. The life that mounts toward God is a power of salvation in the world.

Be true to truth. Love and serve. Stand fast in the sweet and patient temper. Strive upward toward the mountain-summits of spiritual attainment. At last you will be known and understood and loved. At last love and faith will have their full fruition.

Another lesson we should learn from this study. It is the duty of understanding and appreciating others, and sympathizing with them. Often we are guilty of the same indifference and inappreciation toward others as that from which we ourselves suffer. Sometimes our complaints are ungenuine or morbid or even selfish. Your brother does not understand you: do you understand him? Those about you have no sympathy with the best that is in you: have you sympathy with the best that is in them? You long for the word of true recognition and apppreciation from others: do you give them the word of true recognition and appreciation? You are hungry for love and fellowship: but there are many who hunger; what have you for them? The sorrows of Jesus never dimmed his eye to the sorrows of those about him. He understood and appreciated and loved each soul, though he was himself neither recognized nor loved. A single incident out of many vividly illustrates his power to think of others, even in the crisis of his own suffering. As he hung on the cross in the prolonged anguish of dying, he soothed the last moments of an expiring outlaw by his side with words of hope, and made provision for the earthly comfort of his mother by giving the precious charge to a disciple.

We easily grow selfish in our grief or pain; but

the spirit of Jesus in us will ever turn our thoughts outward. We are not understood; let us seek to understand the plain man by our side. We miss the quick and fine appreciation that would make our highest thoughts seem better worth cherishing, and our noblest purposes better worth attempting; let us appreciate the high thoughts that struggle into lame speech, and the purposes that move into imperfect action, in the lives which are about us. We crave in vain the strong and clear-sighted love that would fill our hearts with mighty gladness; let us love the longing souls that thirst and pine for true and tender human affection, within our own little circle.

Sometimes in passionate grief and desire we ask if our fellow-men know us, and we yearn for the response which shall rightly interpret our nature and reconcile our spirits to the vocation to which God has called us. The response may not come here; the reconciling word may not be spoken now; but, like Jesus, under the power of his transcendent example and in the strength of his steadfast spirit, we can live and love and hope and work and suffer and serve, sure that at last we shall not only know as we are known, but also shall be known to the uttermost of our aspiration and purpose, and loved to the full measure of our deep longing, and gladdened with the perfect fruition of our highest endeavor. Meantime we shall have blessed and sustaining fellowship with Him who "came not be ministered unto but to minister, and to give his life a ransom for many;" and in him and in the fulfilment of his mission our life will find its enduring and exceeding great reward.

XIII.

FOES IN THE HOUSEHOLD.

Then to side with Truth is noble when we share her wretched crust,
Ere her cause bring fame and profit, and 't is prosperous to be just;
Then it is the brave man chooses, while the coward stands aside,
Doubting in his abject spirit, till his Lord is crucified,
And the multitude make virtue of the faith they had denied.

. . . .

For Humanity sweeps onward : where to-day the martyr stands,
On the morrow crouches Judas with the silver in his hands;
Far in front the cross stands ready and the crackling fagots burn,
While the hooting mob of yesterday in silent awe return
To glean up the scattered ashes into History's golden urn.

James Russell Lowell.

XIII.

FOES IN THE HOUSEHOLD.

A man's foes will be they of his own household. — MATT. x. 36.

WHEN Jesus spoke these words he was forecasting those experiences into which his disciples must come as the result of the new direction of life that they took from him. Of necessity he was in antagonism to the ruling ideas and conventions of the world in which he moved. He was higher than the men of his time. His spirit was other than theirs. Not unnaturally did Pharisees and Scribes hate him; on the contrary, with perfect consistency, from their point of view, they sought his destruction. The only possible condition of peace between him and them was that he should become like them, — in sympathy with their spirit and ideas, — or that they should become like him. The former was impossible; Jesus turned Pharisee would be Jesus lost from his position as spiritual reformer and Saviour of the world. No abdication and self-contradiction could be more violent and complete than that. The latter was impracticable; the Pharisee turned disciple would be no longer a Pharisee. But the Pharisee was a creature not only of his time but of a long preparatory discipline. He represented the age in his point of view if not altogether in his peculiar opinions. Years and even centuries must pass before Phariseeism could be transformed into the spiritualism of Jesus. Antagonism was therefore inevitable between Jesus and the Pharisees.

Furthermore, Jesus was set, not arbitrarily but from the very nature of the case, in opposition to the dominant spirit of the world. He stood for the great ideas and forces of love, truth, and righteousness. He embodied the spirit that antagonizes selfishness as light antagonizes darkness. Selfishness was intrenched in the habits, institutions, and systems of the race. It was expressed no less in the religions of men than in their social and political customs. It revealed itself no less in their conceptions of God than it did in their estimation of man. To the brute force, the intolerant sensualism, and the tenacious sordidness of men, Jesus opposed his spiritual thoughts of God, of righteousness, and of truth, as they are set forth in the Sermon on the Mount. He was understood by the leaders of society only sufficiently to be hated or despised. His ideas, men felt, as far as they could apprehend those ideas, would revolutionize life and make necessary a complete readjustment of their religious and social relations. In ignorance and in incapacity to understand him, rather than in pure malice, they set themselves against him. He was scarcely using figure of speech, therefore, when he said to his disciples: " Think not that I am come to send peace on earth; I came not to send peace, but a sword."

In proportion as men became in heart his disciples they were aligned to his position. Christianity was the beginning and evolution of a great spiritual and moral reform, — a reform that involved nothing less than the entire, ultimate transformation of humanity. The history of the past eighteen centuries is a history of the struggle of the ideas of Jesus Christ with the instinctive and persistent selfishness of men. We may explain that selfishness as the result of a primeval fall and depravation, or as the survival of primeval animalism which slowly yields to the growing force of the spirit; but, however we explain it, selfishness is the one comprehensive obstruction to the triumph of the Christianity of Jesus.

The disciples of Jesus by their very discipleship were set in antagonism to the prevalent life of the world. Brought by their Master into a new conception of humanity, as well as a new conception of God, and into a new spirit of love and benevolence toward men, they were yet made participants in a fateful strife with the whole world.

As the Jews persecuted Jesus because they did not understand him, and because they mainly felt only the tremendous contradiction, which, both in teaching and character, he presented to their central and most cherished ideas of religion and life; so Jews and Gentiles alike persecuted the disciples of Jesus. The disciples were identified with him. They realized in experience the truth of his saying, "The disciple is not above his teacher, nor the servant above his lord. . . . If they called the master of the house Beelzebub, how much more those of his household!" To prepare them for such inevitable hostility and opposition, Jesus uttered his words of prophetic warning and counsel.

The first three centuries of Christian history were marked by the struggle between Heathenism and Christianity which substantially ended, in the then known world, in the assumption of the throne of the Cæsars by a Christian emperor. Outwardly, at least, there was peace thereafter between the Church and the world, save as strife was precipitated by the political aggressions of the Church. But within the Church the struggle was renewed. The ideas of Jesus were in antagonism to many of the institutions and dogmas that had developed in the Church. The Rome whose head was the pope became even more intolerant than the Rome whose head was Imperator and Pontifex Maximus in one. The simple, sincere, and utterly courageous follower of Christ found his bitterest enemies among those of his own household and of his own communion. Heresy, which early came to mean difference in opinion or belief from formal ecclesiastical and theological standards, was pursued as relentlessly in the Church as formerly the heresy of Jesus was pursued by the orthodox Pharisees. Men killed each other for belief's sake, and thought that thereby they did God service. In many a long and tragical chapter of history we may read the sad fulfilment of Jesus' prophecy.

When the integrity of Roman Christianity was broken by the German revolt under Luther, a new era began. Slowly advanced the emancipation of Europe from the iron grip of Roman Ecclesiasticism. Persecution continued and bloody storms swept over the Netherlands and the Waldensian Valleys and the fair fields of Southern France. But the beginning of the end of organized religious persecution in the Church came with Luther and Zwingle.

In the Protestant Church the old spirit survived and made a history of Protestant persecutions which we read now with a blush of mingled shame and indignation. Always those who have been nearest Jesus Christ in their spirit and purpose, have been farthest from the prevalent ideas and institutions that bore the Christian name.

The progress of society in the mass is slow. Prophetic souls outstrip the majority, and their singularity is punished with misunderstanding, contempt, hatred even, and sometimes death. But the progress of society is sure along the line of

Christ's thought, and each generation, while it persecutes its own prophets, builds monuments to those who were the martyrs of the preceding generation.

With the cessation of physical violence in the attempted repression of divergent religious opinions and convictions, persecution did not cease. It became less brutal, but it continued. The strife was transferred to a higher plane. A man's foes no longer kill him as the Pharisees killed Jesus, as Rome killed the apostles, as the Inquisition killed the Netherlanders and the Huguenots and the Waldensians; but the tongue still stabs, and often more deeply than the knife. Bigotry kindles fires of hate that burn sometimes not less fiercely than the fagot-flames that roared about martyr forms in Smithfield. Jesus is still in advance of the race, and those who press most closely after him must still find bitter verification of those words: "A man's foes will be they of his own household." Thus in the history of the Church we read the fulfilment of Jesus' prophecy.

But that prophecy has a fulfilment of another sort which may claim our attention a moment. Pre-eminently the religion of Jesus is the religion of love — love to God, and love to man. In the teaching of Jesus the love of God and the love of man are inseparable. They are notes that blend in a single chord; they are colors that mingle in a single ray; they are the systole and diastole of one heart.

Love is the law of life. Righteousness is the conformity of action to the impulse and law of love. As long as selfishness exists in the hearts of men, and expresses itself in social customs, and organizes itself in the institutions of political and economic and ecclesiastical life; so long must the strife which Jesus announced, and in his own experience illustrated, continue. The highest life is ever the highest achievement. History seems but the record of a prolonged Passion Week in which the sin of the world is expiated by the ever repeated crucifixion of suffering love. In every soul that suffers for righteousness' sake, for truth's sake, for love's sake, Jesus is seen,

"Toiling up new Calvaries ever, with the cross that turns not back."

They who will follow the Christ fill up the measure of the sufferings of the Christ by which, through the mystery of love and pain, he is redeeming the world.

Is it not true that in the endeavor to live according to the idea and spirit of Jesus Christ, a man's foes are still they of his own household? In society it is the life that is nearest us which often most antagonizes our holiest purposes. In the circle of our most intimate relations spring up the subtlest temptations and the most powerful oppositions to a life in the spirit. The man who would square his life to the law of Jesus, and shape his thinking in utter sincerity by the teaching of Jesus, often must be like Abraham, who, to save his faith in the only God, broke away from the home and society in which polytheism and nature-worship were interwoven with the whole fabric of daily life, and pushed his way across plain and mountain, to a strange land. We need to make, perhaps we can make, no geographical pilgrimage; but in our deepest thought we must journey apart and live in a strenuous solitude.

How often is it the case that a man finds in the narrow circle of his own home and fireside the strongest enemies to that which he sees to be his best life! Sad and tragical enough it is, yet true, that the rough battle-field of the world brings a man into no such crucial trials of his spirit as he sometimes finds in the little sphere of his most intimate relations. Out in the world, amid its tumult and wild strife of brute forces, he wins a victory which, in the seclusion of the home, is wrested from him. Triumphant there, he is baffled and beaten here. Jesus said to the group of disciples that gathered about him in closest intimacy with his daily life: " One of you shall betray me." A Hebrew Psalmist, in an hour of bitter experience, cried out: "Mine own familiar friend, in whom I trusted, which did eat of my bread, hath lifted up his heel against me." Many a soul has tasted the same cup of disappointment and trial — not always through the malice, far oftener through the weakness or the ignorant zeal, of those nearest to him.

Every one in this world is subject to manifold temptations. He who would live toward God, who would increasingly grasp the truth, not as idea simply but as quality and power of life, must overcome the gravitation of his sensuous nature. He must resist the tyranny of those appetites which, controlled, serve, but, uncontrolled, fetter and debase the soul. Whatever associations and fellowships weaken him in this struggle and multiply the occasions and causes of temptation are foes to his real life. The most powerful of these foes are met within the circle of his private acquaintance. Often the very strength of a man is the chief peril of his friend. Often the very security of close companionship is the utmost insecurity from fatal temptation. Only the strongest souls are capable of receiving as well as giving friendships that are at once intimate and wholly beneficent. My weakness may be your peril just in proportion to your love for me. You may stab me to the heart when most you would serve me.

Here is a truth which we do not sufficiently understand. To be a friend is to be laid under sacred bonds of righteousness and sincerity. A recognized enemy puts us on our guard; we lay aside our armor and let vigilance sleep when we enter the circle of those we love. And how many temptations there are that seem not wholly evil. Evil is so mixed with good that it is hard to discriminate, and while we consider and debate we are undone. The foe from afar had assailed us in vain; the foe in our own household has smitten us to the heart.

> "The lie which is all a lie may be met and fought with outright,
> But a lie which is part a truth is a harder matter to fight."

The sin that is part a virtue is the sin that most powerfully tries us and most surely finds our weakness. In a deeper sense than we have thought, perhaps, "a man's foes are they of his own household."

But again, it is not, after all, the common temptations and oppositions to right living that we find on the level of our ordinary sensuous life, which are the most difficult to deal with. He who would live closest to Jesus Christ must share not only the solitude of Jesus, but he must feel the chill and shock of that opposition which springs from the unsympathetic life about him, and the misunderstandings and misinterpretations which often he must bear from those on whose sympathy he seems to have strongest claim. Sympathy, in any deep sense, is possible only where there is community of experience. If one thinks deeply, and rigorously follows his thought into the higher ranges of moral and spritual truth, he must, in so far, draw apart from those who are not given to the same high endeavor. We are set in a certain environment of ideas and customs and sympathies. It is not entirely easy for one to fall below this environment. We are so held by it that it is to us in some sense a conservator of virtue. Some men are not as bad as they would like to be. They are held to a certain decency and morality by the stress of their surroundings. But if it is not easy to fall below the level of the life that is about us, far less easy is it to rise above our environment, — for example to think above and beyond the current thought, to feel more finely than the common sensibility, and to attain a keener spiritual insight than that of those nearest to us. He who attempts it finds oppositions and subtle, unreasoning enmities of which he had not dreamed.

Hence a real rise in spiritual life is both an achievement and a victory. Seldom is the thinker who climbs above the level of contemporaneous "orthodox" opinion congratulated as a pioneer. Often is he first wondered at as singular, then challenged as a transgressor, and then condemned and shot at as a blasphemer and outlaw. Have you not felt, some of you who listen to me, again and again, as you have wakened to a higher perception of truth and a holier ideal of life, and have striven toward that truth, that ideal, — have you not felt the chill of unsympathetic feeling, the rebuff of stolid indifference, the resistance of conventional belief, and the paralyzing touch of misinterpretation, even from some who are nearest to you in social and domestic relations?

He who leaves the beaten path to climb the mountain-side must often walk alone. That were grief enough. But often he must find the hardness of the way made more hard by those who are knit to his heart by many ties.

Who that has striven toward a higher life of thought and action — that has endeavored to press closer to Jesus Christ — but has felt, at some time, the pained astonishment of the soul that cried: —

> "Is it true, O Christ in heaven,
> That the wisest suffer most?
> That the strongest wander farthest,
> And most hopelessly are lost?
> That the mark of rank in nature
> Is capacity for pain,
> And the anguish of the singer
> Makes the music of the strain?"

Deep and far-reaching is the truth of those words which Jesus spoke to his disciples: "Think not that I came to send peace on the earth; I came not to send peace, but a sword. For I came to set a man at variance with his father, and a daughter with her mother, and a bride with her mother-in-law; and a man's foes will be they of his own household." Learning the meaning of these words, we begin to understand also the meaning of these seemingly harder words: "He that loves father or mother more than me, is not worthy of me; and he that loves son or daughter more than me, is not worthy of me. And he that does not take his cross and follow after me, is not worthy of me. He that finds his life shall lose it; and he that loses his life for my sake shall find it."

But let us not think that the truth is a mere disintegrating force, wakening antipathies and producing incessant conflict. Strife must be in order that abiding peace may come at last. Though prophetic spirits take a lonely precedence in the march of human progress, they draw the world after them; though their way here often is the *via dolorosa* of rejection and the cross, at last the cross becomes the sign of final victory, the pledge of a complete redemption of the world, and the seal of a perfected spiritual unity of all men in an eternal fellowship of love and peace.

Thus far I have spoken of the foes which externally assail him who would live the life of the spirit. The words of Jesus: " A man's foes will be they of his own household," are susceptible of an application still more intimate and personal. The greatest battles of life are fought in the arena of a man's own heart. His most powerful and his most insidious foes are within himself. The household of his daily thought and desires and purposes and imaginings contains enemies subtle and strong. In his own bosom the battle must be joined; in his own soul the victory must be won. The solid and significant outcome of life is not the things a man has done, but the something noble and strong and pure which he has become. Character, the product, in some real sense, of our choices, is also the achievement of our inward strifes and endeavors.

"Sure I must fight, if I would reign."

runs the familiar hymn; and this fight, which life is, is primarily with one's undisciplined and untempered self. No temptation from without could touch a man if there were not the temptability within. If "Know thyself" is the counsel of wisdom, "Rule thyself" is the command of righteousness. But often the very qualities and susceptibilities in us that, ruled and chastened, constitute our highest virtues, are also the sources of our greatest peril. The generous instinct of the youthful heart may make but the more riotous prodigal. Imagination, that regal gift, may become

"Procuress to the Lords of Hell."

Sensitiveness to the beautiful may degenerate into the mawkish madness of sentimentalism. And passion that was meant to warm and quicken, may flame into a baleful fire that sears the heart and destroys the soul. There are survivals of animalism and instincts of selfishness in us that must be subdued and extirpated. Here, within, are our subtlest and strongest foes. There is no evasion of these, if we would obtain spiritual manhood and womanhood. They must be overcome. Is this our misfortune?

"No, when the fight begins within himself,
A man's worth something . . . the soul wakes and grows —
Prolong that battle through his life!
Never leave growing till the life to come!"

I have not spoken of the helps — specially the one all-inclusive divine help — which all need who are striving toward the true and the good. Your thought has already supplied this seeming lack in my discourse. The possibility of rising — of overcoming indifference, misinterpretation, and enmity without — lies in the sympathy, the fellowship, the love, and the power of the indwelling Son of God. He who walks with Jesus can walk alone, sure that at last he will have unlimited company. He can bear the sneer of the cynic, the wrath of the bigot, and the coldness of the unsympathetic friend, steadfast in the prophetic faith that truth and love will at last bring the perfect reconciliation. He can resist the stress of temptation, and endure the blows of sorrow through the power distilled from constant divine communion. He can overcome fate itself through the faith which is "the victory that overcometh the world."

So, too, his interior battles he can wage to successful issue because it is God who works in him both to will and to do. The secret of strength is in the revelation of God to and in the individual soul, and in the abiding love and fellowship of him who "of God is made unto us wisdom, and righteousness, and sanctification, and redemption."

XIV.

NOT DESTRUCTION BUT FULFILMENT.

BUILD thee more stately mansions, O my soul,
    As the swift seasons roll!
    Leave thy low-vaulted past!
Let each new temple, nobler than the last,
Shut thee from heaven with a dome more vast,
    Till thou at length art free,
Leaving thine outgrown shell by life's unresting sea!
                  OLIVER WENDELL HOLMES.

XIV.

NOT DESTRUCTION BUT FULFILMENT.

I came not to destroy, but to fulfil. — MATT. v. 17.

MY purpose at present is to elucidate the principle that underlies these words, rather than to show their historic fulfilment in the action and teaching of Jesus both during his public ministry and during the centuries that have elapsed since his ascension.

Jesus did destroy very much, but destruction was not the end at which he aimed. His purpose was to plant, to quicken, to upbuild. However much he took away, he put more and better in its place. If he destroyed men's trust in legal observances, he drew them to a rational and efficacious trust in God. If he destroyed traditions, he gave vital truths. If he destroyed institutions, he gave power to construct other and better institutions.

He was not a mere iconoclast, but a builder. His spirit is the most powerful constructive force in history. He whom the Pharisees both hated and feared as the destroyer of religion, re-created religion and gave it a place and power in the world beyond the prevision of all prophetic dreams.

In this particular of planting and developing, Jesus is the supreme exemplar, as he is in so many other ways. We need to study this aspect of his character and work to-day, when the tendency to destroy is so powerful, when there is such impatience with the old and the over-worn. On every side, in the Church and in the State, there is a growing discontent with that which has long exercised the authority of custom. The social order is challenged and questioned, and here and there its overthrow is both urged and attempted. The dogmas and forms of the Church are subjected to close and ever severer criticism, and criticism is steadily pouring itself into action.

" The old order changeth, yielding place to new,
And God fulfils himself in many ways,
Lest one good custom should corrupt the world."

The present time is marked by a powerful movement for reform that invades all fields, — political, religious, and social. Those who lead in this rising enterprise are mainly the young; not merely the young in years, but the young in mind and spirit. I would not say one word, if I could, to check the movement. It is a sign and product of life, and God is in it. The world is still inchoate and undeveloped. Humanity is yet in its spiritual childhood. There is more truth than men have yet taken into consciousness. There is a better social order than we have yet attained. There is a holier Church than has yet appeared. History is but the slow unfolding of God's purpose, and every advance is a fuller revelation in terms of thought or organic civilization of God in his world.

But the time is one of danger and temptation; and I would, if I could, speak a word of counsel, especially to the young. The tendency to destroy is deep laid in our nature. Man is both conservative and destructive. He is usually destructive in his youth and conservative in old age. It has been wisely remarked that the conservative is only the radical gone to seed. The history of religious thought strikingly illustrates the truth that the conservatism of to-day was radicalism yesterday; just as the radicalism of to-day will be conservatism to-morrow. The transition from the one to the other which time and growth effect is becoming more rapid. What strides have been made in twenty years! Twenty years ago the doctrine of evolution was heresy in nearly every pulpit and theological seminary; to-day it is almost, if not quite, the main formative principle of philosophical theology, and has its advocates and expounders in innumerable pulpits and in half the theological schools in the land. Indeed the phraseology of evolutionary thought is unconsciously employed by many who are not aware that they have moved forward with the moving planet into fuller light.

The tendency to destroy, I say, is deep-laid in our nature. It is the instinct of the child. He delights to smash things. We may analyze this instinct into (1) *curiosity*, the desire to see inside of things and know how they are made. Give your watch to your child, and he will, if he can, break it open, to see the wheels go round. He cuts open the bellows to see where the wind comes from. The little girl dissects her doll in order to penetrate the mystery of its form.

This instinct of destruction is partly the expression (2) of the child's pure *delight in exerting force*. He lives mainly in his senses and loves to feel himself in contact with things. There is for him an experience of triumph and a glow of exultant joy in his small demolitions. His impulse is not bad. The careful and anxious parent thinks it an evidence of depravity, but it is not; it is only the upleaping of the nascent power within him that, by and by, if not misdirected, will appear in the energy of the inventor, the trader, the builder of railroads and mills, perhaps in the creator of immortal poems, or pictures, or stately systems of philosophy. That which makes the child's destructive instinct seem bad is his lack, through ignorance, of any true appreciation of values. To the child things seem to come easily and he naturally makes them go easily. He has not yet learned that construction is a slow and costly process. By and by he will learn it, perhaps in painful ways, and thus will discover his true function in the world.

The young man has the same impulse, qualified indeed by his larger knowledge, but still full of menace to the existing order of things. As he comes in contact with the world he finds customs, institutions and rules of life that seem to him " fair game " for the exercise of his destructive energy.

In the first place, he has a strong sense of undefined power, and an inherent love of struggle. As boys often fight " for the fun of it," so young manhood pours out its energy in belligerent ways for the sheer sake of overturning something that by its very immovableness seems to challenge him.

There is in youth, too, an immense capacity for ideals. Often it is full of instinctive chivalry. Some things seem wrong and restrictive of the finest life. The ardent young knight sees only the palpable obstruction, and not its causes and the reasons of its being; and he runs atilt upon it with frank resolution to overturn it and put it out of the way.

This instinct appears when the young and vigorous mind is confronted by traditions and dogmas. That a dogma may be the slow growth of centuries does not abash him. He questions everything. He would question gravitation and the multiplication table if they stood in his way. Political constitutions, social customs, commercial methods, everything, is answerable to the eager inquisitiveness of his spirit. Most interesting, because in some respects most important, is the attitude of awakening mind toward religion, especially as religion presents itself under the form of creeds and religious ceremonies and institutions. There is in the awakened mind of youth a lack of that disciplined reverence which comes only from long experience. There is impatience of limitation and mystery, and there is a fine egotism. There is also the temptation to use power for the sake of its mere exercise and the temptation arising from the sense of importance which power to attack and destroy gives. This last temptation is not confined to youth. Some men are always in the opposition because thus only can they make themselves felt and draw attention to themselves. The smallest power can obstruct. The littlest mind can delay if it cannot effectually hinder progress. He who has not force to draw the load onward, may stop its advance by blocking the wheels. The temptation to do this, however, seldom assails youth, for youth is generous, if rash; it rather attacks the old, than obstructs the new.

In such a time as the present there is a tremendous temptation to young men to be iconoclasts. They have the zeal of the men in the parable who would rush into the field and tear up the cockle and other weeds, regardless of havoc to the wheat. For example, they confound a questionable theology with all theology; a doubtful custom with the human need that created the custom; and an outgrown institution with the organic law and tendency of human life.

I will specify that you may see exactly what I mean. The crass doctrine of prayer, which makes the ignorance or whim of the creature direct the power that administers the universe, is seen to be obnoxious to sound reason, and there is a tremendous jump at once to the conclusion that prayer is fruitless and even absurd, or else that it is merely a spiritual gymnastic exercise. A certain doctrine of atonement is seen to be repugnant both to intelligence and morality, and the inference is drawn that there is no vicariousness in Christ's life and death or in the character of God. The theory of the verbal infallibility of the Sacred Scriptures manifestly is untenable, and therefore it is assumed that there is no inspiration and no certain revelation of the divine will in those Scriptures. The Church is seen to be deeply marked by the defects of human nature, and the conclusion is hastily reached that the Church has no supreme value and authority. These roughly sketched specifications are sufficient to illustrate the tendency and temptation that work in many minds. Acting in such ill-considered and hasty ways, and ruled by the iconoclastic temper, the mind makes havoc of the most substantial and precious treasures of human life.

Now it must be admitted that destruction is

necessary to progress. Errors and abuses, the heritage of long years, grow into vast burdens and obstructions. They must be abolished. The pioneer's axe must destroy the forest and make way for agriculture and civilization. The quartz in the mountain must be crushed that the gold may be extracted. So old custom must be broken up that a better order may prevail. Slavery and serfdom must be destroyed, even at the cost of numberless human lives and fortunes, that liberty may be realized. Superstition must be slain that reason may rule and pure faith may live. Wrong ideas must be overthrown and imprisoning forms must be shattered, that truth may nourish the soul and pure piety may sanctify the life.

But while all this is true, there are other things that are also true. Let us consider some of these. (1) Destruction is easy, and, of itself fruitless; while construction is difficult and costly and slow. It is easy to do mischief. A child can burn a palace which requires many crafty men and many months of labor to build. A boy can wreck a railway train which takes many hands and much skill to construct. A malicious tongue can work harm in a few minutes which years of life can scarcely repair. Yes, it is easy to destroy, and the ambition merely to pull down and demolish is, of itself a low ambition.

(2) Destruction, necessary as it is to progress, may be premature. A man's religion may be

fetishism; but it is the best he has. Better that than none at all, for the lowest form of religion keeps alive the religious susceptibility of human nature, and that susceptibility is the spring of the noblest character as well as of the greatest happiness. "Though it be true," said Lowell, "that the idol is the measure of the worshipper, yet the worship has in it the germ of a nobler religion." To destroy the savage man's fetichism without giving him something else that is better is to rob and injure him.

(3) Destruction is best accomplished by construction. I know that some evils and errors of man must be overcome by stern and relentless conflict. I know that sometimes only volcanic upheaval is able to loosen the roots of gigantic wrong. But there is a lesson for us in the fact that most of the transformations in nature, in the geologic history of the globe, are the result of slow and silent forces. The millennium of silent growth and change accomplishes far more in making the habitable earth than many cataclysms. The method of nature and of nature's God is to crowd out the old by the growing force of the new. If the old leaves in the wood cling to the twigs beyond their time the new growth pushes them off in the spring.

(4) It is nobler and more beneficent to be a builder, a creator, than it is a puller down and a destroyer. The pages of history are full of the

names of men who have ravaged kingdoms, and burned cities, and furrowed fair lands with graves. But the Muse is rewriting her annals. Already history is telling the story of the constructors and creators rather than of the destroyers. It is a noble and pure ambition that urges men to plant and fashion, to change evil custom by instituting a good custom, to supplant the old faith with the new.

Let me ask you to apply these truths, first of all, to your own personal life. Each of us has defects and evils in himself to overcome. The problem of self-reform and self-development is largely a problem of method. Take the matter of evil habits into which you have fallen. How shall you deal with them? You will not deal with them most successfully by a mere *tour de force*, — by a passionate and sudden revolt. Destroy an evil habit by promptly cultivating a good habit. Oppose to the bad force a good force, and utilize the habit-making tendency of your nature in the formation of habits that are wholesome and pure.

Then, in the matter of thinking, when you find, or reasonably suspect, that ideas which you have held are mistaken, do not at once throw your whole intellectual nature into revolt and exhaust your strength in criticism and attack. Seek to supplant wrong ideas by right ideas. Instead of merely combating error in yourself or in others, strive to discover and grasp truths. Open your minds freely to the instructions of the holiest and the wisest men whom you know. There is no real help for you in the camp of deniers and scoffers. Be patient, and be hospitable to every gleam of truth that may come to you from nature or the experience of men. If you are lost in a dark cave the way to do is to move toward the light, and not to fight the darkness until at last in disgust and despair you are ready to deny that there is any sun.

In the matter of the affections, expel a base love by cultivating a pure love. There is no power in sheer will to cast out of the heart a polluting occupant comparable with the expulsive force of a new and exalting passion. Apply this principle to the whole of life, — to companionships: seek the good while you abandon the evil; to books: devote yourselves to the great and pure, while you turn away from the vulgar and corrupting; to occupations: busy your energies with helpful tasks while you forsake the unworthy or mischievous; and to thoughts: extrude the low and frivolous and sensual by addressing your minds to the noble and refined.

Let me ask you also to apply the truths which we have been considering to your related life, to your social and public activities. (1) Seek first and always not to destroy, but to plant, to build, and to create. "Any beast can do mischief;" it is man's high prerogative to do good. Every one can add something to the intellectual and moral as well as to the material values of life. A good life is the best argument for righteousness. It is much more difficult to work constructively than it is to attack and demolish, and it is not nearly so likely to bring notoriety; but it will accomplish infinitely more, and it will dignify your whole life in the eyes of the world as well as in your own consciousness. (2) Destroy by superseding the false with the true. In the Church, supplant dead formality, not by an iconoclasm that issues in formlessness, but by filling existing forms with new life, and thus modifying forms to meet the changing exigencies of the ever growing soul. Supplant outgrown dogmas, not by throwing theology overboard and by dogmatically denying all creeds; but by producing better expressions of truth already known, and by striving after the attainment of higher truths.

The anarchist in the social realm has his counterpart in the religious realm. The anarchist would destroy all society and government, so the radical would destroy all objective religion. But, as beneath the defects and abuses that mark social and political life there is a solid and enduring treasure of righteousness and law, so beneath all the errors and faults of creed and Church there is a solid and enduring treasure of goodness and truth. Neither the anarchist nor the radical is the true reformer. The true reformer works constructively.

He does destroy, but destruction is incidental to his aim. He builds more than he demolishes, and plants more than he uproots.

The process of true reform is so slow, so difficult, and so costly, and there are so many hindrances to progress presented by human stupidity and selfishness and moral and intellectual inertness, that he who contemplates the enterprise of bettering human life is beset by the temptation to give up, to let things remain as they are, and to draw apart in indifference or cynicism; or to grow impatient and shatter things, to break down and destroy indiscriminately.

Resist both temptations. Believe in progress and improvement. Seek persistently the larger truth, the purer form and the higher state. Let abolition and destruction serve the beneficent, constructive purpose. The process begins within. "Make the tree good and its fruit good." Strive to free your minds from bondage to errors which are half-truths by moving onward into the fuller truth. Follow Jesus Christ, the true Reformer. Work along his lines. Love God and your fellow-man. Believe in the good purpose of God and the good possibility of mankind. And make your life one constant endeavor to hasten the perfect salvation of the world and the perfect evolution of the kingdom of God.

XV.

THE JOY OF THE LORD.

For only work that is for God alone
Hath an unceasing guerdon of delight,
A guerdon unaffected by the sight
Of great success, nor by its loss o'erthrown.
All else is vanity beneath the sun,
There may be joy in *doing*, but it palls when *done*.
              Frances Ridley Havergal.

XV.

THE JOY OF THE LORD.

His Lord said unto him, Well done, good and faithful servant; thou hast been faithful over a few things, I will make thee ruler over many things; enter thou into the joy of thy Lord.—MATT. xxv. 23.

THE first thing that strikes us as we read this parable is that the reward is given to the faithful, and it is the fidelity of the servant, not the amount of results achieved by him, that attracts and measures the reward. We are very apt to think of this parable as having application only to the end of our earthly life, and as indicating the divine judgment upon our entire career. Undoubtedly it does refer to the conclusion and final outcome of our earthly life, but that by no means exhausts its meaning. We are prone to push off to the end of the world the application of a good many of Christ's sayings. For example, how many there are still who think of "the coming of the kingdom" as a remote future and climacteric event, instead of being, as it is, the process of human history and the present and continuous fulfilment of the divine will. Jesus said:

"The kingdom of God is among you;" it is here, though we may not see it. In thinking of the parable now before us, we are apt to give an exclusive prominence to the idea of the second coming of Christ, as suggested and illustrated by the coming of the Lord to make a reckoning with his servants. Of course there is an element of truth in this view, but it is not the whole truth, nor is it even the largest truth. There are comings of the Lord in the present time, and reckonings with his servants now; there are also promotions for faithfulness and punishments for recreancy. In the continuous experience of human society these are not always discernible by human eyes, especially if they have not been trained to look deeply into life and to judge it from the spiritual point of view. Yet it is possible to see, again and again, exemplifications of Christ's teaching concerning the divine judgment on our life in the experience of our fellows and of ourselves. Many a humble soul is advanced to higher work because of conspicuous faithfulness in that which is lower, and many a soul is dismissed from high service, or reduced to a lower order, because of unfaithfulness.

We must remember that the servants in the parable are not discharged from duty, as if they had reached the end of their service, but the faithful are promoted to larger service. This is full of suggestion. "He that hath, to him shall be given." He that does the work set to his hand will find other work adapted to his enlarged capability. We have here an illustration of a permanent principle in the divine administration of life. The promotion to larger service is the reward of fidelity. This is distinctly implied in the words, "Thou hast been faithful over a few things; I will make thee ruler over many things." But a further reward is suggested in the words, "Enter thou into the joy of thy Lord;" and this reward is no more to be referred exclusively to the remote future than is the promotion to higher service.

Certainly the "joy of the Lord" will be found in the ultimate glorious fruition of the Lord's great enterprise, to which the faithful servant has contributed. We may legitimately look forward to that as the soldier looks forward to the final triumph of his leader and his cause, and the establishment of perpetual peace; but the "joy of the Lord" is found also here and now, and continuously, in the higher work and the greater capacity and the closer fellowship with the Master which are attained by faithfulness. This, after all, is the immediately important truth — faithfulness has its reward in the present life, both in weightier trusts and in a deeper entrance into the purposes of God. Just here is disclosed to us the meaning of great trial and severe struggle which the soul has borne with fidelity. God is educating us to larger capability for work and larger capacity for appreciating his nature and understanding his purposes with man.

There is, then, a "joy of the Lord" which is discovered in faithful work or faithful endurance, as well as a "joy of the Lord" into which we shall enter as the final reward of earthly endeavor and experience. The thing of chief importance is fidelity; that underlies everything. "He who is faithful over a few things," says George MacDonald, "is a lord of cities. It does not matter whether you preach in Westminster Abbey or teach a ragged class, so you be faithful. Faithfulness is all."

But the special thought that I would have you consider now is the "joy of the Lord" actually discovered and experienced in the service of God. This reward and accompaniment of faithfulness is not postponed; it is not artificial; it is not the factitious rapture of the ascetic saint; it lies in the direct line of true development, and is the immediate and continuous product of sincere and patient endeavor.

It is a familiar truth that man finds a real and hearty pleasure in action; not merely in exercise, though the use of limb and faculty in health is always pleasurable, but in action that is effective. That is, there is a real pleasure in any sort of true accomplishment. Matthew Arnold said: "It is undeniable that the exercise of a creative power, that a free creative activity, is the true function of man; it has proved to be so by man's finding in it his true happiness." The truth is suggested in these words, but it is neither adequately defined nor is its full significance indicated.

To make something is the delight of the healthy child, boy or girl. The pleasure found in action increases in proportion to increase in fulness and range of power. The great part of the joy of life is found in ever accomplishing something. We make too much, oftentimes, of the attractiveness of mere objective reward. If work is rational and progressive it always has a charm. In no sphere may this be seen more clearly than in that of the education of the young. Pestalozzi and Fröbel were right in their belief that education should always be a pleasurable process to the child. For a long time it was considered that studies were valuable in proportion to their repulsiveness to the student. Instead of following Shakespeare's maxim, "In brief, sir, study what you most affect," teachers were disposed to say to a pupil who complained, for example, that he did not like mathematics: "Then that is the very study that you ought to pursue;" and, indeed, the study of many subjects was often made repellant by the method in which they were taught. We are beginning to learn at last that pleasure in work is not inimical to the efficiency of the work, but, on the contrary, it increases that efficiency. Many of us find an image of ourselves in childhood in

> ". . . the whining schoolboy, with his satchel
> And shining morning face, creeping like snail
> Unwillingly to school."

But now it is becoming the rule rather than the exception that children like to go to school and find a real joy in their work.

Human activity is meant to be pleasurable. We know from experience that there is a pleasure in simply doing something. The sense of mastery over objects and forces, and the sense of achieving the ends which we set before ourselves, give a real elation to life. But action must have a true end; fruitless or aimless endeavor soon loses its charm because the action itself is not progressive. In actual achieving, however, there is a stronger attractive force than the mere desire for the result of our labor. For, in the first place, we do not and we can not pause contented over results. We plan for ourselves a certain task and think that we shall be content when it is is achieved; but when we arrive at the proposed end, when we attain the certain contemplated result, we quickly begin to look ahead for something else to engage our interest and to draw out our powers.

Take a familiar example from our every-day life. The desire for wealth apparently is the strongest desire which actuates many men. But why is it that when men have acquired wealth enough, and more than enough, to satisfy all reasonable wants they still keep on striving for more? The mere money, or even that which money can buy, is not sufficient to explain the persistent ardor of the pursuit. There are men, I am sorry to say, who have become so sordid that their whole desire and endeavor seem to terminate on lucre. But there are very many others of whom this is not true. In the case of these it is not the wealth, but the struggle for wealth, which is the chief attraction. The fascination of effort and achievement increases even while the attraction of the result lessens.

But we are all familiar with the delight that is found in mere achievement, that is, not simple effort, but effort that accomplishes. The bustling housewife finds a keen pleasure in exorcising the demons of disorder and dirt; the activity, if not carried to the point of exhaustion, is pleasurable. The healthy artisan finds a joy in his daily activity, in using tools and producing fabrics. The student delights in the play and strain of his faculties and in winning, one after another, the objects of his research. The naturalist, like a Darwin or an Agassiz, discovers continuous happiness in pushing far and wide his investigations into nature and in drawing forth her curious secrets. The artist glows with pleasure in the mere effort by which the creatures of his imagination are wrought out and fixed in paint or marble. The inventor tastes a pure delight in the strenuous intension of mind out of which are born new contrivances for the advancement of industry, or the increase of human comfort.

Now, the depth and purity of our pleasure in

achievement increases as our work rises into the higher realms of action, and as it calls into exercise the higher faculties of our nature. The artist has a finer pleasure in his work than the mere artisan, unless the artisan is also an artist in his sensibility. The pleasure of activity rises in quality and in intensity also as our work rises into endeavor for moral ends. There is a purer and a greater pleasure in the pursuit of truth than in the pursuit of wealth. When truth is sought that men may be enlightened there is a still further rise in the joy of endeavor.

The apprehension of moral ends and the effort to attain them raises the pleasure of action into happiness. It is not merely in creative effort, as Matthew Arnold suggested, but in creative or productive action along moral and spiritual lines, that man finds his true happiness. The philosopher, the poet, or the artist may be sad in proportion to his very power, but the philanthropist, the true, strong lover and server of mankind, is a man of joy.

This, then, is the main thought to which I would lead your minds now. If the mere sense of achieving gives delight, how much greater and purer is the delight when the sense of achieving is animated by love, — when the sense of achieving rises into the consciousness of accomplishing that which benefits and blesses others. There is no satisfaction in work for its own sake, or in the objective rewards of work, that is comparable to that pure pleasure, that sweet exultation of the soul, which labor and self-sacrifice for the good of men always produce. Man tastes the blessedness of God in unselfish work for man.

Take it on the lower plane of service, that, for example, of ministering to the simplest material needs, such as feeding a hungry family. How strong is the sensation of pleasure that comes to us as we divide our store of food with those who have none! Suppose you have a friend or an acquaintance who is involved in financial trouble and, though it be at the cost of considerable sacrifice, you furnish the means of setting him free from his embarrassment, how surely the very reflex of your deed brightens the day about you and gives a new zest to life. Perhaps at some time you have had the good fortune of rescuing some one who was in imminent peril of death; perhaps you have saved his life at the risk of your own life. I venture to say that nothing which you have ever accomplished in the line of material achievement has given you so much satisfaction, a joy that so constantly abides with you, as that deed has done. In deeds of ministry like those which I have named there is great joy, not merely in the result but in the very action, and this joy is sweet just in proportion as it has no alloy of selfishness.

If we ascend to the still higher plane of spiritual

help and service to men, we find that such service opens up for us new phases of experience in pleasure. Suppose that, with the quick insight of love, you discover a man who is in a fateful grapple with some mighty temptation. It seems as if he must sink down in defeat and you come to his rescue with your words of encouragement, your sympathy with his nature and condition, your understanding of his experience, and your faith in God and in him. The struggle is long and difficult; you enter into it so deeply that you feel the tremendous strain in your own soul, and so experience a sort of vicarious passion for the man; but at last the effort is successful; the evil is overcome, and the man stands, shaken and breathless, but saved, and saved through you. How blessed has been the endeavor! How strong and pure is the joy that bathes your whole being.

Suppose, now, that instead of helping one who is consciously in trouble, you give yourself to the task of waking up a soul for the first time to a sense of life's real meaning and purpose. Suppose that you give yourself to the effort of bringing him to a knowledge of God and of all that it means to be a child of God, and become thus a savior to him; you have achieved the divinest deed possible for any one in this world, and tasted the sweetest bliss this side of heaven. I do not know why I say this side of heaven, for heaven itself can offer no greater gladness than that which is found in being a savior. There is no joy like that.

But such service as I have described is not easy; it is not accomplished merely by words. It involves labor of mind and spirit; often one must enter into the very agony and passion of Christ himself.

To be doing good in the higher realms of human life, to be helping men in the spirit, is the most rewarding endeavor in which it is possible for us to engage. Life brings to us nothing so valuable as the capability and the opportunity for such ministry as this. No material rewards of labor, no external rewards that can be conceived of, have the sweet and strong fascination of the mere effort itself to serve our fellow-men in the spirit, when we are really giving ourselves to this effort, and strongly putting forth our powers in self-forgetfulness and self-sacrifice for the blessing of men. The joy that was set before Christ, on account of which, the writer of "Hebrews" tells us, he "endured the cross despising the shame," surely was not merely a future and remote blessedness that should come with the full accomplishment of his redemptive purpose. It was, rather, the joy of saving the world found in the very effort to save it.

But the experience of the "joy of the Lord" is not confined to the highest and most spiritual spheres of human effort. Something of that joy comes into every human heart that is simply seeking to do good. Every deed of help to men, every act of pure self-sacrifice, every ministry however humble, opens some channel for the inflowing into our life of the divine gladness. Our lives are made miserable by our selfishness, often when we least suspect it. The best medicine for our own sorrows is the effort to heal the sorrows of some one else. However heavy our personal trials may be, we shall forget our quarrel with life and with God if we will give ourselves steadily to the endeavor to make life brighter and fuller of comfort and blessing to others. So deep and persistent is this truth that at last it is getting itself formulated even in the scientific interpretation of the world. Evolution, which has seemed to us so pitiless a process, with its appalling "Struggle for Existence" and its "Survival of the Fittest," is having to-day a larger interpretation, and men are discovering that the strongest force in the evolutionary process is not the "Struggle for Life" but the "Struggle for the Life of Others."

Deep in the very springs and sources of all life is planted the impulse which is working itself out in innumerable ways through all the rise of life from protoplasm to man, and from man to the Christ, and has its supreme expression in the cross of immortal love and divine self-sacrifice.

Now the Church exists peculiarly for the salvation of men. How much that means it is difficult to put into a few words. It certainly means far more than we have been in the habit of conceiving.

All good that we can do to men is included; all improvement of life; all rescue from imperfection, physical, mental, and moral; all charities and ministries of love to the needs of men's hearts and spirits as well as bodies; all achievements of reform; every betterment of material and intellectual and moral condition, — all these are included in the process of salvation. All ends and efforts that are discerned by love and dominated by spiritual purpose are comprehended in this great enterprise. In accomplishing this manifold work, by its fundamental appeal to the moral sense and its characteristic ministry to the religious needs of men, the Church is fulfilling its mission, and in fulfilling its mission it enters into the joy of its Lord. Too much has the Church sought its joy in being the object of God's saving purpose; there is a nobler joy than that; it is attained in the consciousness of being the means of God's saving purpose. Higher and better than being saved is being a savior, and to this experience and endeavor the Church of Christ is pre-eminently called. Too often the Church has folded its hands and sung its hymns in complacent delight over its own redemption, meanwhile its real redemption was farther away than it dreamed. Jesus said: "He that saveth his own soul shall lose it." The business of the Church is not to save itself, but to save the world, and in saving the world it is to find its true blessedness.

My brethren, you are in the Church not merely

to get good, but to do good; not merely to be comfortable in the consciousness of your own acceptance with God, but to give and to serve in sympathy with the spirit and purpose of him who is the Head of the Church in order that he may be the Saviour of the world. The achievement of the world's redemption is to be brought about through the body of Christ, which body ye are. Look this truth in the face and see what it means. Try to make out some of its clear and unescapable implications that must come home "to our business and bosoms." Your work as Christians, as members of the Church, the body of Christ, has a double focus; it terminates on two vitally related ends: (1) The salvation of individual souls, — a work that demands individual effort; and (2) The salvation of the collective soul, or society, — a work that demands, with individual effort, the corporate action and devotion of the Church. The thought is large and can be only suggested now. To awaken individual souls and bring them into acquaintance and fellowship with Jesus Christ; to help them to see the spiritual significance of life and to press forward into the realms of spiritual experience, — that is one part of the work. In that work each individual Christian, in one way or another, may successfully engage. Every one of us has some power, as every one of us has some opportunity, to touch with spiritual quickening some other life. Many of us think that we cannot do this by speech; we shrink from approaching people on the religious side by means of personal address; but we forget that to do this is easy and its significance is slight, compared with the positive ministry in which we should engage by striving to live according to the spirit of Christ. No man can so much help me to faith by talking to me about faith as he can by visibly living a life of faith. No one can so strongly assure me of the comfort for my sorrow that there is in God as by himself visibly finding comfort for his own sorrows in God. No man can so powerfully move me to self-sacrifice for the good of others as he who illustrates that self-sacrifice in his own conduct. There is possible for every one of us a larger ministry to individual souls than we have yet attained; and in that ministry, if we can once crucify our selfishness, we shall find a pleasure richly compensating us for our labors and pains.

But our work terminates not only upon individual souls, but also upon society. To leaven society with the spirit of Christ, so that its laws, its customs, its business methods, and all its enterprises shall conform more and more to the law of love, and to do this by living on a high level of conscientious and unselfish citizenship and by consciously seeking the improvement and spiritualization of the organic life of the community, — this is but another part of the same work; it is the logical sequent of the salvation of the individual soul. Here, too, we are pressed by the temptation to shirk our duty and to ignore our privilege. Here, too, a false modesty keeps us back from exerting our full power, and even from doing many things our ability to do which we are ready to acknowledge. The presence of evil in the political administration of society and in social customs and activities is due not merely to some ineradicable, malevolent spirit in society, but to the unfaithfulness of those who know the right and neglect to do it, those who have the knowledge of virtue in its springs and sources and fail to act fully according to the knowledge, those who are called by God to be the saviors of the world and are failing perhaps to save even themselves through their failure to fulfil the mission committed to them to be the saviors of humanity.

This entire work of individual and social salvation from sin and ignorance and selfishness and misery, — in a word, this great work of creating the spiritual kingdom in which life shall find its true fulfilment, — is the work which God has appointed us. To this enterprise we are bound by all the love and authority and majesty of Christ; to this we are bound by every sentiment of gratitude and every mandate of duty; to this we are drawn by the attraction of that "joy of the Lord" which is sweeter than the bliss of Paradise and as deep as the unsounded abyss of the love of God. This is my message, nay, may it be the Spirit's message, to you to-day. Recognize and welcome the service to which you are called. Seek to bring some soul to God; seek to help upward some one who is down; seek to make the life about you better, more humane, more cheerful, more in harmony with the law of Christ. Seek and find the joy of the Lord by faithfulness in doing His will; you will find it as surely as you give yourself to this divine endeavor; and then you will need no testimony from prophet or apostle to prove to you the real blessedness and the real triumph of life.

XVI.

THE NEED OF PATIENCE.

EXPERIENCE, like a pale musician, holds
A dulcimer of patience in his hand
Whence harmonies we cannot understand,
Of God's will in his worlds. The strain unfolds
In sad perplexèd minors. Deathly colds
Fall on us while we hear and countermand
Our sanguine heart back from the fancy-land
With nightingales in visionary wolds.
We murmur, "Where is any certain tune
Or measured music, in such notes as these?" —
But angels, leaning from the golden seat,
Are not so minded: their fine ear hath won
The issue of completed cadences;
And, smiling down the stars, they whisper, "SWEET."
ELIZABETH BARRETT BROWNING.

XVI.

THE NEED OF PATIENCE.

For ye have need of patience, that having done the will of God, ye may receive the promise. — Heb. x. 36.

THERE is something to be done which often is difficult and sometimes painful; that is the will of God, constraining and guiding us through manifold duties and trials. There is something to be received which is beautiful and precious; that is "the promise," coming to fulfilment in the completion of our lives in blessedness and power — "a better possession and an abiding one." There is also something necessary to the doing God's will and receiving the promise; that is "patience." We might summarize the text in three words — patience, obedience, fulfilment. The whole Christian life is comprised in these three words; indeed, a very large part is comprised in the two words, patience and obedience.

Our immediate concern is with the first of these. The Greek word, ὑπομένω, means "to stay behind when others have departed," as brave and faithful soldiers obstinately maintain their ground when the weak and cowardly have run away. It means also "to bear up under, to endure." The noun ὑπομονή, which is used in the text, is somewhat inadequately translated by "patience," derived from the Latin word, *patior*, meaning "to suffer." What is patience, in the Christian sense? It is not mere stoicism, the power to bear grimly and uncomplainingly because one must. Trial thus borne may sour the whole interior life. Nor is it mere listless resignation, a helpless yielding to the inevitable. It is cheerful, sweet-spirited endurance. It is meeting difficulty and bearing pain and accepting trial in such a way that these heavy experiences are conquered and turned into sources of increased strength and beauty and fruitfulness of life. It is not merely steadfastness under trial, but it is the steadfast abiding in right and gracious moods, through all experiences.

Christian patience is nourished by Christian hope. In a large, unselfish way it ever has respect unto "the recompense of reward." It is rooted in faith in God. Moses endured "as seeing him who is invisible." Jesus, "for the joy that was set before him, endured the cross despising the shame." The promise of the divine fulfilment of life underlies and feeds and justifies the patient endurance of life's tragical and as yet but dimly understood discipline.

The apostle, writing to scattered Hebrew Christians, who were subjected to persecution as well as to many temptations, says: "Ye have need of patience." He tells them that they need patience for two distinct yet inseparable reasons. The *first* reason is, that they "may do the will of God." He does not mean that they must first have patience, and then they may do the will of God; but, rather, that they have need of patience in doing the will of God; still, the complete obedience toward which they are to strive is to be attained only through patient endurance. The *second* reason for patience is, that they may receive the promise. The goal and crown of life has its legitimate and powerful attraction. One does not run a race for the sake of going from here to there. One does not hew out a road that leads to nothing. There is a kind of talk about the selfishness of looking for reward that wearies one with its shallow sentimentality and its utter lack of appreciation of life and its aims. Doubtless many men are selfish in their expectation of future reward; but their fault or vice does not justify one in denying to life any end commensurate with its desperate struggles, its Promethean agonies, and its mighty hopes.

Let us then consider *the need of patience.* To accept and progressively to fulfil the will of God as the regnant principle of life requires of us patience. In common usage "the will of God" means sometimes that divine purpose which comprises in itself the whole aim and movement of God in human history. Sometimes it means the universal law of righteousness which is revealed to us both in the sacred Scriptures and in the moral constitution of man. More specifically it is used to express the regulative principle of holiness which is the ground of obligation and the guide of conduct in the individual life.

With respect to the individual soul, the will of God is both moral requirement and benevolent purpose. It concerns both action and character. It contemplates both what we shall do and what we shall become. God demands that we shall do right and he intends that we shall be right. In his letter to the Ephesians, St. Paul exhorts them to be servants of Christ, "doing the will of God from the heart." In his letter to the Thessalonians he says: "This is the will of God, even your sanctification," where his meaning evidently is not only that it is God's command, but also that it is his beneficent intention, that they shall become holy. Thus, "the will of God" indicates both a direction to follow and a destiny to fulfil. Obedience is not merely the conformity of acts to specific moral and ritual precepts, but far more it is response to a spiritual attraction. The will of God is to be done, but it can be done only as character as well as conduct comes into harmony with that will. We do the will of God not only when we obey his mandates, but also when we submit to his purpose and consentingly suffer it to guide our thought and rule our feelings and mould into symmetry and beauty our entire life. God's will is mandatory but it is also purposeful, for his love, quite as much as his sovereignty, is in his will.

1. In the first place, then, the will of God *is something to be done;* and we who are required to do that will "have need of patience." We have need of patience because God's will is difficult to do. Nothing is more certain than that to a soul struggling out of the bad habitudes of a sordid and selfish life righteousness is not easy. "If any man wills to come after me," said Jesus, "let him renounce himself and take up his cross and follow me." Have you found that easy? Is it not a slow and painful and sometimes a seemingly futile struggle? The best life inevitably is the most difficult, until it is achieved, until it becomes

> "the natural way of living."

When I say that to do the will of God is difficult, I do not mean that God lays arbitrary and needless exactions upon us, for he does not. Sometimes, indeed, he seems to us to do so, for we are very ignorant and often very foolish. Sometimes, too, we mistake the exactions of men for the exactions of God. The Pharisees laid heavy burdens and grievous to be borne on men's shoulders. There are always those who are quick to identify their notions of what we should do with the divine commands. The progress of mankind into liberty is slow because of "the zeal without knowledge" that so often characterizes those who assume the right to speak for God.

It is not true that God ever designedly sets a hard task for us that he may thus put us through some sharp expiation of our sin before he shows us any favor. The difficulty of doing God's will lies mainly in us — in our self-will. Sin is the enthronement of self over life. Righteousness is the enthronement of God over life. The step from the one to the other measures an enormous revolution, and the complete transition involves a vast moral growth and discipline. When a man is "converted," — to use a word that is continually and harmfully misused, — when he turns consciously toward God, his nature is not at once entirely transformed. The controlling principle and tendency of his life are changed, but, beyond that, his nature lies like a rude and rebellious province that must be conquered and civilized and disciplined into loyalty and liberty. There is in human nature much tough resistance to the rule of the spirit. The passions are hot and imperious. The imagination is lawless. The heart is full of low desires and a strong impatience of any authority save that of its own lusts.

Now the divine method is not to crush human individuality and to compel the soul by irresistible force. Character is the product of choices. Holy character is the product of holy choices. God is seeking in men the development of character; hence his method is to secure in them the rise and triumph of free choices against the imperious demands of selfishness and the gravitation of animalism. His requirements are always beneficently inflexible. There is no laxity in his purpose. There is no accommodation of the ideal to human weakness. Accommodation, the lowering of moral requirement to our condition, would defeat the very end which is infinitely desirable, that is, the deliverance and development of our natures out of weakness and imperfection. In many merciful and educative ways God does accommodate himself to our ignorance and ineptitude; but there is no lowering of the ideal standard. That can never descend to us; we must ascend to it.

It follows, then, that while we are imperfect, our efforts to do the will of God are made at some cost to our ease and pleasure, and are accomplished with difficulty. For many, in the beginning of the spiritual life, every holy choice costs the death of some unholy choice; every volition of pure love comes into action at the expense of some selfish volition. Our endeavors after righteousness are in the line and are the sequent of a voluntary subjection of our natures of God. Sanctification is God's work in man, but it is achieved through man, the various human powers and capacities being the channels through which divine grace operates. We must do God's will, if at all, consentingly, and by overcoming the dissent of our sinful dispositions. The Christian life thus demands in us alertness and a strenuous persistence. And just here rises the need of patience. It is hard work to school the will into quick obedience to righteousness. It is difficult to subdue the flesh, and cast out pride and envy, and compel our selfish hearts to the service of love. One often grows weary of this internal fight, even though it is "the good fight." Sometimes, too, the special requirements of God are difficult to understand. Our desires sometimes seem needlessly crossed. Often, according to our low ideas of gain and loss, obedience is very costly. Well, righteousnsss is costly, else it were not worth much, — scarcely worth the toil and pain of that blessed life, eighteen hundred years ago, through which God supremely disclosed the ties that bind humanity indissolubly to himself.

Thus far I have spoken only of the internal difficulty of doing God's will, that difficulty which inheres in our ignorance and weakness and selfishness. There are difficulties also that belong to our circumstances. The drift of life about us often is away from holiness. There are temptations to evil self-indulgence that spring upon us from without. There are obstacles to be overcome in our temporal condition and relationships. God's will must be done sometimes in the face of misconception and ridicule and even pugnacious opposition.

The difficulty of faithfully doing God's will often is complicated and increased by the character of one's necessary associates who are indifferent to spiritual things and perhaps even godless; sometimes by the nature of one's business, as when fidelity to the right puts in peril, or even sacrifices, the hard-earned fruits of years of toil. In many ways and through the action of many causes we may find it difficult and costly to hold steadfastly to righteousness. The quality which the Christian then most needs is patience, — the capacity to suffer and bear and hold fast that which is good, —

> "One equal temper of heroic hearts,
> Made weak by time and fate, but strong in will
> To strive, to seek, to find, and not to yield."

Yes, higher than the noble pagan stoicism which the poet has voiced in these lines, is the virtue which the Christian needs, the patience that grounds itself in an obstinate faith in God and an unflinching devotion to righteousness.

2. In the second place, the will of God *is something to be borne.* Let us never forget that God is not so much seeking our service as he is seeking us. What we do is important, but mainly because it is fruitage and advertisement of what we are. The divine will does not terminate upon a certain kind of human conduct, but rather upon a certain condition and quality of the human soul. God is making men. Hence the adjustment of our lives is such as to develop us in certain graces and strengths of character. I do not doubt that God wishes us to be happy. For this very reason, in

part, he wills that we shall become holy. Life is a trial of faith, a discipline of love, a schooling in service. It is manifestly ordered so as to secure the largest and best results in character. This view of life can be got, however, only from the divine point of view. All earthly conditions, from one point of view, take on the aspect of tests. We call this life a probation, that is, a proving, a demonstrating of what quality the soul is, and what capability it has of spiritual culture. But from another and higher point of view, life is not so much probation as it is education. The change of emphasis on these two words indicates more clearly perhaps than any other single thing the fundamental change in religious thought which has taken place in our day. The prophetic mind of Lessing, a hundred years ago, saw that the real significance of Hebrew history, and of all history, lies in this, that it witnesses to a divine education of humanity. What is true of humanity is true also of the individual soul. In a sense, every man is on probation; but in a deeper and broader sense, every man is undergoing a process of education of which probation is an important element; or, to use an expression now familiar to our ears, he is undergoing a process of evolution from lower to higher. The world is not a court-room, but a school-room, and "our school-hours," as Carlyle said, "are all the days and nights of our existence."

Now God's will as something to be done must be

obeyed under the conditions determined by God's will as something to be borne. Do not get the hard and unjust notion that the Heavenly Father takes one child here and plunges him into a hissing bath of affliction, and another child there and thrusts him under the harrow of pain. To a large degree we make our own environment; this plainly is a part of the divine plan. We are schooled out of sinful disposition by being permitted to let loose upon ourselves the retributive forces of natural penalty. We are taught wisdom by the smiting recoil of our own folly and perversity. But there is vastly more in our life, as a plan of God, than this. It cannot all be analyzed and explained here. This much, however, is clear; a large part of life is of a sort to work us out of all placid contentment and slothful ease.

God's will, then, as the regulative principle of life has to be done under frequent oppressions of sorrow and pain, through subtle or tumultuous assaults of temptation, and against stubborn difficulties. There are the perplexities and doubts that rise both from imperfect knowledge, and from a relatively low moral state. The unchastened heart breeds more doubts than the puzzled mind, and doubts too of a deadlier sort. There are the multitudinous frictions and raspings of daily contact with men and things, — exasperating complications in business, worrying cares in the household, disappointments of cherished hope, the balking of purposes that, apparently, have been the main threads on which our life's aspirations and efforts were strung. And, with all these, there is the constant pressure of the strong currents of selfish and worldly life which surround us. Some of these external conditions we are unable to change, except as we conquer them by developing a spirit superior to every circumstance. This is exactly what we are meant to do. If we present to our untoward surroundings a steadfast patience, that patience itself becomes an armature against all attacks that would disturb our peace. And then, too, God's will, working itself out in ways of discipline, moves toward its beneficent end, — the strengthening, beautifying and perfecting of our souls in holy character.

St. James uses language on this matter which undisciplined and sensitive souls can hardly understand: "My brethren, count it all joy when ye fall into divers temptations," that is, experiences that test the temper and the faith, as well as solicitations to evil, "knowing that the trying of your faith worketh patience. But let patience have her perfect work, that ye may be perfect and entire, lacking nothing." Patience — steadfast, brave endurance — is the grace or quality of soul by which free course is given to the action of that divine will which is accomplishing our full salvation.

The apostle says: "Ye have need of patience that ye may do the will of God." So, every day,

The Need of Patience.

God is bidding us to be patient. Life is often a hard struggle. It is a militant campaign, and many a day is marked by a hotly contested battle — a battle that has not always resulted in victory for us. The swiftly passing years bring many cares and perplexities. Few are the days that have not their nettle-like irritations. Then there are days of heavy, tyrannous pain. There are losses for which there seem to be no compensations. There are graves along our pathway, some of them so fresh that the grass is not yet green above them, — graves in which lie buried loves and perished hopes. How many a man

"bears a laden breast,
Full of sad experience, moving toward the stillness of his rest."

But to all the Master is saying: "Be patient; what I do thou knowest not now, but thou shalt know hereafter. Prove all things; hold fast that which is good. Be steadfast, immovable, always abounding in the work of the Lord; for this is the will of God, even your sanctification. My grace shall be sufficient for thee. Be of good cheer: I have overcome the world."

It is possible for one to live in this world and be glad in spite of temptation and care and loss. It is possible to live in such a temper that sorrow shall be powerless deeply to agitate the heart. It is possible for us to attain a spirit of such purity and strength that God's disciplining will shall be borne without outcry and wild storm of tempestuous feeling. It is possible to be superior to the thousand petty anxieties which each day would thrust upon us; to overcome the frictions and irritations of business and domestic experience; and to expel from our griefs their bitterest element. But it can be done only by living persistently in the higher ranges of our nature. It is when we dwell in our lower moods of temper and feeling that we are conquered and tormented by anxiety and temptation. When God bids us be patient, then, he is but urging us up to a higher, sunnier plane of life; drawing us out of our bondage to circumstance, and bidding us to come into that constant fellowship with himself in which the soul finds resources that are in no way subject to the accidents of time and place and possession. Stoicism says: "Be sufficient for thyself; then thou shalt be above circumstance, not elated by prosperity, nor depressed by adversity." Christian Patience says: "Let God be thy sufficiency; hearken unto him; then shall thy peace be as a river, and thy righteousness as the waves of the sea."

Christian patience, unlike mere stoicism, is the product of trust in God, and confidence in the soul's divinely assured future. Be patient, O Christian, and in the darkest hour of this present time thou canst say to thy soul: "Hope thou in God: for I shall yet praise him, who is the health of my countenance and my God." Believe in God and hope in God, and a whole tumultuous sea of sorrows cannot rob you of blessedness.

We have need of patience in order that we may both do and bear the will of God; but experience demonstrates this, that sincere and persistent endeavor to do the will of God, begets in the heart a power of cheerful and victorious endurance. It is not the one

> "Who does God's will with a ready heart,
> And hands that are swift and willing,"

who is fretful and anxious, and full of complaints; who is gloomily or petulantly resistant to the discipline of divine Providence. Faithful obedience turns every cross into a throne of power and illumines every cloud with a bow of promise.

3. *Finally:* Patience in doing the will of God has its inspiration and its crown in the promise of God. This is the justification of patient service, that it has its final issue in a completed redemption. The troubled stream of life is at last to flow out into an immeasurable breadth of clear, sunny, everlasting calm. The long, stressful conflict will end in a triumph the fruits of which no lapse of ages can exhaust, and a peace the perpetuity of which can never be broken.

"The promise" is the pledge of God's deep interest in men; therefore it is the support of faith, the food of hope, and the inspiration to patient endurance. The Christian life is not a doubtful enterprise. God himself has something great at stake in our salvation. The completed redemption for which the ages have waited will at last appear.

Strive to be great in patience. Do God's will zealously; bear his will bravely. Let sorrow come, and disappointment, and care, and pain; they are divine ministers whose work is to discipline you in wisdom and to develop you in beauty and strength. The longest day of toil and strife ends at last, and after toil comes rest.

> "Under the fount of ill
> Many a cup doth fill,
> And the patient lip, though it drinketh oft,
> Finds only the bitter still.
>
> "Truth seemeth oft to sleep,
> Blessings so slow to reap,
> Till the hours of waiting are weary to bear,
> And the courage is hard to keep.
>
> "Nevertheless I know
> Out of the dark must grow
> Sooner or later whatever is fair,
> Since the heavens have willed it so.
>
> "After the storm a calm;
> After the bruise a balm;
> For the ill brings good in the Lord's own time,
> And the sigh becomes the psalm."

XVII.

THE WAY TO HEAVEN.

O Thou great Friend to all the sons of men,
Who once didst come in humblest guise below,
Sin to rebuke, to break the captive's chain,
And call Thy brethren forth from want and woe:

We look to Thee; Thy truth is still the light
Which guides the nations, groping on their way,
Stumbling and falling in disastrous night,
Yet hoping ever for the perfect day.

Yes! Thou art still the Life; Thou art the Way
The holiest know; Light, Life, and Way of heaven!
And they who dearest hope, and deepest pray,
Toil by the Light, Life, Way, which Thou hast given.

THEODORE PARKER.

XVII.

THE WAY TO HEAVEN.

I am the way, the truth, and the life. — JOHN. xiv. 6.

IN that wonderful discourse beginning with the words: "Let not your heart be troubled: believe in God and believe in me," Jesus was preparing the minds of his disciples for experiences that were sure to come to them in the days when he would be no longer with them. They could have had, at the time, only the dimmest idea of the great meaning that weighted his speech and made it rich enough to tempt and reward centuries of exploration. Much that Jesus said was for future, rather than immediate, use. His full meaning could appear only when experience, that master-teacher, should develop capacity and give point of view. Yet, as the conversation went on, the disciples must have had some glimmering of his meaning; they must have felt that his words reached beyond the present and shot a beam of light into the far future. Certainly the Church has found in these words clear intimations of heaven and the heavenly life; and we must read them in this sense, under the conviction that Jesus meant them to be a help and a guide to his followers, in succeeding times, in their thinking about death and the hereafter.

Whatever ideas the disciples had of heaven were, doubtless, crude and limited, and the locality and outward conditions of the future life rather than the subjective quality of that life engaged their minds. Heaven was to them a place of rest and of happiness in the fruition of their hopes.

Jesus, at the outset, found a common ground for their thought and his. Heaven is a place. "In my Father's house are many mansions;" that is, heaven is an organized home-life and social-life. But the idea of place is at once subordinated to the idea of state or condition. Heaven is a fellowship and an experience, a realization of highest life. The succeeding words make this clear, for they reveal the unbroken continuity between the life of the soul here in this world and the life in the world to come.

But let us pause a moment to note a peculiar and persistent characteristic of Jesus' teaching; it is the central place which he gives himself. "Believe in God, and believe in *Me*. . . . If it were not so *I* would have told you. . . . *I* go to prepare a place for you. . . . *I* come again and will receive you unto *myself*. . . . Where *I* am there ye may be also. . . . *I* am the way . . . No one cometh unto the Father, but by *me*." It is an extraordinary feature of Jesus' method that he puts himself before his followers in this way. Yet there is nothing monstrous about his vast assumption as there would be if it were made by any other man. We cannot help feeling that this is the eminently natural thing for him to do; not simply because we are used to the idea of Jesus' pre-eminence, and reverently familiar with his manner; nor because it is a necessary involvement of some theory of his person that he should claim pre-eminence; but because of our involuntary, almost instinctive, recognition of his transcendent personality. From the first moment he justifies himself to our hearts. His confidence and calm authority are irresistible; we trust him because he is sure of himself. If he were not so sure of himself and of his necessary relation to men; if he spoke doubtfully or with hesitation; his power would be gone.

There is great significance in this. Such a method must have reason in fact. And, indeed, experience proves that departure from this method of Jesus is followed by failure in the attempt to bring men to him. Let go of Christ as central in the redemption of the world and you let go of the chief power by which men are moved toward the spiritual life.

Let us return now to the conversation. Jesus is

speaking of heaven; the disciples are vaguely groping after his meaning. He says: "Whither I go ye know the way." Thomas exclaims: "We know not whither thou goest: how know we the way?" Thomas' thought terminates on place rather than on state. Jesus' answer makes plain that he is speaking of himself as the way to heaven, not in the sense simply of a means to a place, but rather in the sense of a means unto a life. The idea of a heavenly life — a character and experience — dominates his whole thought. He says nothing of where, save in the words: "I go to prepare a place for you," and "Where I am, there ye may be also;" but he speaks explicitly of how: — "I am the way." The thought is difficult but the succeeding words aid us: "I am the way, the truth, and the life." — I am the heavenly way, the heavenly truth, and the heavenly life. The goal of life, both here and hereafter, is not simply a locality, a place, arrival at which is the end of the way. Place is not fixed, limited, and final. The dominant idea is that of state, character, quality of life; and to this the idea of place is constantly subordinated.

The disciples thought first and mainly of place and circumstance. We are very prone to the same way of thinking. Many of us, indeed, are almost as limited in our thought as they. We "want to go to heaven" because heaven is a place of ease, of freedom from toil and sorrow; in a word, a place of satisfaction to our desires. It is still something to have, rather than somewhat to become. Like children, we think that there we shall be rid of what is irksome and disagreeable, and shall obtain what we covet.

Undoubtedly under this crude conception there is a certain truth. But how immovably Jesus holds our thought, as he held the thought of his disciples, to the central truth, that the goal of life is not possession but experience; not things and circumstances, but capacity and power; not a place, but a condition and quality of life.

As the kingdom of God has its beginning here, and unfolds toward its future perfection of order and beauty, — manifesting itself through all the spheres and relations and activities of earthly life, — so heaven has its beginning in present character and experience. The way, which Christ is, is the process of unfolding our natures, under his influence and tuition, into heavenly dispositions and capacities, of rising into heavenly experiences, of putting forth heavenly activities, of appropriating heavenly fellowship, and of reaching toward heavenly ideals.

We think only, or mainly, of shaking off the present, with its burdens of care, its fetters of habit, its necessities of self-denial, its pains and sorrows and discontents, and of springing at one bound into the full enjoyment of perfect blessedness; but we cannot shake off the present. It is part of us and we of it. Within it, as in a chrysalis, we are fashioning the future. Heaven is for the heavenly mind, the heavenly taste, and the heavenly capacity. There is a truth in the Hindoo doctrine of the transmigration of souls; or, in other words, that doctrine is the caricature of a truth. The Hindoo believes that the bestial man goes into a bestial body; for example, the glutton into a swine, the cruel and bloodthirsty man into a tiger. The truth is that we are now, in large degree, determining our future environment.

All life here is meant to be a schooling toward heaven, so that heaven shall come but as the blooming of the bud into the flower. We talk of preparing for heaven as of preparing for a journey; but preparing for heaven is developing the heavenly spirit and capacity by present growth in all those qualities of mind and heart and soul which make the beginning of a heaven on the earth. If love were supreme, we sometimes say, heaven would be begun. It is true. We experience what we are fit for, here and hereafter.

In answer to Thomas' question: "Lord, we know not whither thou goest; how know we the way?" Jesus said: "I am the way, the truth, and the life." These words give us a strong intimation, not to say revelation, of Jesus' idea of heaven. That he identifies heaven with knowledge of God and life in Him is evident from the added words: "No man cometh unto the Father, but by me." He is not laying down an arbitrary condition. Jesus stands for the spiritual mind by which alone personality approaches God; and the way to God and into the life of God is the way to heaven and into the heavenly life. God is the heaven of the soul; the fulness of life in God is the heavenly life. "It is not in heaven that we are to find God," said Godet, "but in God that we are to find heaven." Ah, but how unreal and difficult all this is! And how disappointing to our spirits, still so deeply immersed in the senses, still so crude and untempered! Yes; but there lies the truth. Heaven is not lowered to our present moods and capacities and tastes; we are to be lifted up to the heavenly state by the discipline and purification and enlargement of our natures; and that is the process of salvation.

Thus the words of the text begin to disclose their meaning. "I am the way" into the life of God; so must we interpret Jesus. Now, in what sense can we say, must we say, that Jesus is the way to God and into the life of God? Certainly not in the sense that he purchased God's love for us; for his whole mission is declared to be the result and expression of God's love. "God so loved the world that he gave his only begotten son." Not in the sense that he took away any barrier in the mind of God to mercy and forgiveness toward men; for such a barrier, did it exist, would be a barrier to the love itself of which Jesus' coming was the supreme expression. Men have often crystallized their doubt of God's love into the very theories of atonement by which they assumed to show how that love could be efficacious in saving sinners.

Yet the way which Jesus is, is a way for God as as well as a way for man.

1. *It is a way for God* (1) of self-disclosure. It is the way of infinite love into the sphere of the finite. To human beings God must reveal himself in human ways; that is, through human personality, character and action. He does so reveal himself in and through every soul in proportion to each soul's capacity to receive and express him. The greatest soul is the best medium of revelation; through Jesus, therefore, the revelation is pre-eminent. In him the love of God expresses itself, pours itself forth, and finds instrument for the execution of its purpose.

"The way" is thus also, (2) a way of power. The self-disclosure of God is a self-communication. In Christ God touches man, secures a real and efficacious contact with his reason and conscience and affections. Christ is "the power of God unto salvation." "In him was life, and the life was the light of men." He said: "I am come that ye might have life;" that is, not mere respite from death; ye have not yet begun to live. I am the quickening power which makes you alive unto God.

2. The way which Jesus is, is also *a way for man.* Jesus is (1) the way of knowledge. We know God through him. The universe, as a means of revelation, is vague and enigmatical, compared with personality. It is personality alone which gives us the key to the interpretation of the universe. We read the laws of the world through the rationality of our own minds. The groping of the soul — "feeling after God, if haply it may find him," — becomes, in its perception of Christ, the laying hold of God which is eternal life.

(2) It is, therefore, a way of approach. The life-giving touch of God in Christ makes possible and actual the movement of our souls to the Father. Jesus Christ, in himself, — his words, his deeds, his character, his spirit, the totality of his life, — discloses the way to God. As the type and exemplar of man, he shows himself to be not merely a way, but the way, into the heavenly life and experience. *First:* By his exemplification of faith. In him we see what faith is; what that exercise of the soul comprises. His immediate, continuous apprehension of the Father illustrates his own word: "The pure in heart shall see God." *Second:* by his exemplification of obedience. Here is the clear exhibition of man's true subjection to the divine. This is no stoical endurance of bondage to a hard and inscrutable fate, but the free acceptance of an inviolably good and righteous will. In him obedience is response to a divine attraction. *Third:* By

his exemplification of Sonship. It is a concrete living expression of filial confidence, glad reverence, and sweet fellowship. This is the way of the heavenly life; it is not a didactic rule, or formal description, but the very life itself. Although on earth, in the midst of earthly engagements and experiences, he is still "the Son of Man who is in heaven."

Interpreted by the living personality, faith in God is, for us, the frank acceptance of the divine good-will toward us, and, in the conscious experience of the divine life and love, the discovery of all that we need — pardon and cleansing from sin, motives to holiness, and power to achieve the life of the spirit.

Obedience to God is the disciplinary regimen by which our lives are shaped into habits of righteousness. This is very different from doing something in order that we may be saved. It is the free response of the creature to the Creator, the disciple to his Master, the child to his Father. It is the actual and progressive experience of salvation by the unfolding of the divine life in the soul.

Sonship to God is the conscious entrance into the filial relation to the Father, personal communion with him and joyous participation in his thoughts and purposes; it is the experience of confidence, love, aspiration, hope, expectation, content, blessedness.

Faith, obedience, realized sonship — this is the

way which Jesus is and into which he would draw us. There is no other way. There is no heaven save for the heavenly life. And the heavenly life is not postponed to some future time and place, to be attained by the magical efficacy of physical death; it begins here and now. We have entered that life already in just so far as we have entered into the spirit of Christ. "If any man hath not the spirit of Christ, he is none of his." Nothing takes the place of this emergence of our souls from the death of sin into the life of the spirit; in this is the full meaning of salvation.

But Jesus said also: "I am the truth." We must follow the same vital method of interpretation as that which we have followed in studying him as "the way." The meaning of these words is far more than that he spoke the truth. He is the truth. Truth is not merely a matter of knowledge and correct ideas; it is a quality of life. Its highest form is not to be found in propositions or statements of doctrine, but in being, — in character and life. He who truly receives Christ receives more than the dogmas of the Church, and more even than the didactic utterances of the Scriptures.

> "Beyond the sacred page
> I see Thee, Lord."

It is extremely important to know what is true. It is a great achievement to grasp the truth as statement of fact or principle. But it is a much greater achievement to attain unto truth of being — to become the truth.

All spiritual truth, as distinguished from what we call "natural truth," that is, truth of natural facts and relations, is capable of full expression only in personality; in other words, truth has its ultimate end, not in knowledge, but in being. It matters little that we know many truths, if we ourselves are untrue. Jesus was not using a figure of speech when he said: "I am the truth." Being "the truth," he was in right relations to all being, — to God, the trustful, obedient son; to men, the loving brother, the powerful helper, the enlightening teacher, and the perfect Saviour. In him love and righteousness, the vital elements of truth as quality of being and life, attained full embodiment.

It is this which makes Jesus the type of what we are to be. Here is the goal of our aspiration, — not simply to know, but to be; not to stop, content with having grasped certain principles which commend themselves to us as true, but to reach forward toward the full embodiment of divine love and righteousness in our characters. "Every one that is of the truth heareth my voice," said Jesus. He means: He that hath entered into this experience, in which truth is no longer held as a possession external to the thinker's self, but in which it has become incorporate with his very being, so that thought and will and speech and deed are true, — are the faithful and inevitable expression of his innermost spirit, the very effluence of his character, — he heareth my voice and knoweth me as true.

Rising to this conception of truth as quality of being, as belonging to the very substance of our spiritual life, we rise far above the dusty arena of debate. Opinions are of little weight compared with " truth in the inward part." Our thinking is no longer at variance with our action. Our hopes are no longer dissevered from the main enterprise of our daily life. Our unity with our fellow-men ceases to be a mere agreement of superficial ideas or customs, and becomes a solidarity of soul in the life of God revealed and embodied in Christ, and henceforth revealed and embodied in us. Herein is the true unity of the Church — the Church which ultimately is to be the redeemed humanity — in which the one life of God shall pour itself forth in limitless variety of beautiful and harmonious expression, the symphony of a spiritual universe.

In conclusion, I dwell for a few minutes on the words, " I am the life." This entire saying of Jesus is cumulative in meaning. The meaning unfolds in the successive words, " way," " truth," " life."

The way of faith, obedience, and realized sonship leads into truth as quality and power of being, and the soul, thus informed with truth, experiences the reality of life — that divine self-conscious energy in the possession of which man knows and feels himself in God. This is the life eternal. This is salvation, not as a hope, merely, but as an experience.

Thus the heavenly way leads into the heavenly life by a spiritual process in which the incarnation passes over from an object of thought into a fact of experience, and God manifests himself in his children. Thus man becomes a "partaker of the divine nature," and thus is fulfilled the prayer of Jesus and the purpose of God: — " that they may be one, as we are one; I in them, and thou in me, that they may be perfected into one."

In this experience man becomes at last himself also "the way, the truth, and the life," and the heavenly state fulfils the heavenly aspiration and the heavenly discipline. Then heaven is attained, — not a mere place, nor a mere state of fixed and dead uniformity, — but a power, an experience, and a life, in which the invisible and eternal God ever more and more completely fulfils and expresses himself in the thousand-fold harmonies of a spiritual cosmos, the radiant centre which is the Son of God, the archetypal man, the beginning and the end of the creation of God, the glorious Redeemer and Head of humanity in whom the Infinite Soul finds concrete and personal manifestation to all finite intelligences.

But while the thought of heaven as a state and quality of spiritual life is the dominant thought in the teaching of Jesus, and while we need to inform our minds and chasten our desires and correct our aspirations and aims by this thought, it does not exclude the idea of locality and relationship and activities. Heaven is a place. There life will rise toward its fulfilment on every side of our capacity and need. There friends, long severed from each other, will meet with mutual recognition. There the tears of sorrow will cease to flow. There toil will not weary, and care will not harass, the soul. There all creative powers will have full scope. There, as here, we shall find engagement for every essential faculty of mind and hand. I would not impoverish the thought of heaven; I would enrich it rather by showing that heaven is worth all the long struggle and tragedy of earthly life, worth all aspiration and endeavor, worth all that Calvary can mean to man and to God. But I would strip away all selfish and deceitful hopes. Heaven is for the heavenly mind; it is the blossoming and fulfilment of the heavenly life, begun here in weakness and sorrow and conflict with doubts and fears and temptations, but sought and won by the way of faith in God and earnest striving after that holiness " without which no man shall see the Lord."

Often those who endeavor most diligently to live the heavenly life have least consciousness of success and least confidence of obtaining the heavenly crown; but the faithful, though often baffled and cast down, though often too blind with tears or too faint with striving to see anything save to-day's duty and to-morrow's approaching mist of death, will surely find a satisfying fulfilment of life's prophetic aspiration in the presence of Him who said:

"I go to prepare a place for you. And if I go and prepare a place for you, I come again, and will receive you unto myself; that where I am, there ye may be also."

"O happy soul! be thankful now and rest;
 Heaven is a goodly land,
And God is love, and those He loves are blest.
 Now thou dost understand;
The least thou hast is better than the best

"That thou didst hope for. Now upon thine eyes
 The new life opens fair —
Before thy feet the blessed journey lies
 Through home-lands everywhere,
And heaven to thee is all a sweet surprise."

THE END.

THIRD EDITION.

THE AIM OF LIFE.

Plain Talks to Young Men and Women.

By Rev. PHILIP STAFFORD MOXOM.

One volume. 16mo. Cloth. 300 pages. Price, $1.00.

Of this book, the *New England Journal of Education* says: "Under the title of THE AIM OF LIFE, Rev. Philip S. Moxom addresses to young people a series of plain, practical talks upon influences that are to be met, contended, or redeemed every day. The essays evince a keen yet sympathetic observation of young manhood and womanhood, and an appreciative regard for its foibles, the force of its environments, and above all, of its possibilities of achievement. That possibility of achievement, and the means thereto, derives a forceful significance from being made the subject of the first essay and the title of the book. Having thus laid stress on his principle, the author forbears to lift up beautiful ideals in the hope that their intrinsic merit shall draw all men unto them, but rather he endeavors to incite the noble instincts that practical every-day life must either foster or annul. Such titles as Character, Companionship, Temperance, Debt, The True Aristocracy, Education, Saving Time, Ethics of Amusement, Reading, Orthodoxy, show the scope of the theme, which, if varied in expression, is one throughout all. The essays are not sermonic: they emphasize the power of Christianity; they recognize at the same time the power of personality. Christian ethics expressed in plain, forcible language, and innocent of didacticism, young people always appreciate. Such are Dr. Moxom's essays, originally given to the public as addresses to young people in Boston and Cleveland. Now their publication, in convenient form, it is to be hoped, seals their value with permanency."

The Independent says: "Of course it is a good book for young people to read, especially in the view given of character as the supreme result of life."

The Review of Reviews says: "The chapters are marked by a high moral purpose and a direct, vigorous utterance."

The New York Tribune says: "But he presents the old truths in such a vivid and picturesque way, clothing his thoughts, moreover, in such forcible and nervous English, that the most apathetic reader will be stimulated by a perusal of the thirteen chapters that compose the volume."

The Springfield Republican says: "They have a degree of attractiveness quite unusual in volumes of homiletics."

The Outlook says: "The scholar's hand is visible on almost every page, and the way in which etymology is made to yield illustration and exposition of the leading ideas of the successive addresses is both a noticeable literary merit and extremely effective as a method of instruction."

Dr. Moxom's Books.

SECOND EDITION.

FROM JERUSALEM TO NICÆA.

The Church in the First Three Centuries. (Lowell Lectures.) By PHILIP STAFFORD MOXOM, author of "The Aim of Life." 12mo. Cloth. Price, $1.50.

CONTENTS.

1. THE RISE AND SPREAD OF CHRISTIANITY.
2. THE ORGANIZATION OF THE EARLY CHURCH.
3. THE APOSTOLIC FATHERS.
4. THE STRUGGLE WITH HEATHENISM: PERSECUTIONS.
5. THE STRUGGLE WITH HEATHENISM: THE APOLOGISTS.
6. THE STRUGGLE WITHIN THE CHURCH: HERESIES.
7. THE CHRISTIAN SCHOOL OF ALEXANDRIA.
8. THE FIRST ECUMENICAL COUNCIL.

The book is strongly written. It moves on from starting point to goal with life and vigor, everywhere revealing the signs of broad and comprehensive study and of the firm grasp of material. It must rank its author among the men who have brought to the teaching of history not only the best results of the scientific method, but an enthusiasm and power that make the past as real as the living present. — *Standard*, Chicago.

In its picturesque pages are brought before us the great fathers of the Church, the fierce struggles and martyrdoms of those heroic days. — *Golden Rule*.

The general reader who desires a compact yet comprehensive and intelligible view of this early period of Chistianity, can find no better book for his purpose than this interesting volume. — *Christian Work*.

Readers of this book will gain a pretty thorough general knowledge of the rise and spread of Christianity, the organization and development of the early church, the Apostolic Fathers, the persecutions, the Apologists, the struggles with heresies, the Christian School of Alexandria, and the First Ecumenical Council. — *Chicago Advance*.

This is an entertaining as well as instructive book by Philip S. Moxom. It comprises a series of lectures on Christianity, delivered by him under the auspices of the Lowell Institute in Boston last March. Each lecture illustrates some particular phase of the growth of Christianity, its birth with the advent of Jesus of Nazareth to the first ecumenical council held at Nicæa, A. D. 325. The struggles of the early Christians, the frightful persecutions to which they were subjected for holding the belief that Christ was the Redeemer of the world, the contest with heathenism and the church, the story of the great discussion which led to the formation of the Nicene creed, viz., faith in the trinity of the Father, Son, and Holy Ghost, are told with great power. Mr. Moxom's book is one that will recommend itself to every student of religious history, for its depth and breadth and its loftiness of style. — *San Francisco Bulletin*.

The World Beautiful.

By LILIAN WHITING.

AFTER all, it rests with ourselves as to whether we shall live in a World Beautiful. It depends little on external scenery, little on those circumstances outside our personal control. Like the kingdom of heaven, it is not a locality, but a condition . . . [Pp. 11 and 16.]

"The World Beautiful" comes only to those with thoughts beautiful and acts in keeping therewith. The human mind impressed with the duty of human happiness as an every-day duty is quickest to see that it comes surest to those who give happiness to others. It is thus the great agent of unselfishness, which uplifts and exalts the race and brings heaven down to the homes of the earth. These essays, elegant in their literary work, without dogma or an effort at preaching, strike the chords that bring the sweet music to the human soul. In addition to the leading essay, from which the little volume takes its name, there are four others, viz: "Friendship," "Our Social Salvation," "Lotus Eating," and "That Which Is to Come." The last named is a beautiful rehearsal of life's possibilities. The little book will be enjoyed by every thoughtful Christian reader, and to others it may possibly awaken a new train of thoughts, and very certain it is they will be pure and good. — *Chicago Inter Ocean.*

It shows that the writer has risen into the clear atmosphere of truth, and it appeals constantly to the sympathies of men and women who recognize their duty and are glad of sympathetic words to help them in discharging it. This book will greatly increase the esteem in which she is held, and it reveals an ethical purpose and a spiritual power which are tempered by a considerable knowledge of the world. Miss Whiting has put rhetoric to one side, and her readers will gladly recognize that simple truth is her utmost skill. What she has to say on the relations of friendship is very beautiful and very true, and the sincerity pervading these pages is not the least of their attractions. — *Boston Herald.*

Such winning words of deep belief in the best, which is accessible to all of us, make friends of the reader at once, and he must be a rare person who does not lay down this unassuming volume with a feeling that he has been helped to live his life more generously and kindly than before. — *Literary World.*

The charm of freshness and simplicity in their treatment, . . . they go straight to the mark, and that mark a high one; they are thoughtful, and can but be hopeful. — *Advertiser.*

NINTH EDITION.

16mo. Cloth, $1.00; white and gold, $1.25.

At all Bookstores.   Postpaid, on receipt of price.

ROBERTS BROTHERS, Boston.

Messrs. Roberts Brothers' Publications.

ETHICAL RELIGION.

BY WILLIAM MACKINTIRE SALTER.

One volume. 12mo. Cloth, Price, $1.50.

The familiar saying about the prophet and his own country is freshly illustrated by Mr. William M. Salter, of the Chicago Society for Ethical Culture, whose works might be called for in vain at most American bookstores, and which are yet translated into German, and in Germany everywhere, as Mr. Edwin D. Mead writes, exposed for sale. . . . We, for our part, will say that the compliment done Mr. Salter in the recognition of his earnest and thoughtful work is richly deserved. — *Chicago Dial.*

He [Mr. Salter] is a man of eloquence and earnestness, as these discourses show; and their translation into German evinces their power to commend themselves to a much wider constituency than that to which they were first addressed. — *The American.*

There is not a little to commend in this volume. It inculcates a lofty morality, and is far above the level of the utilitarian and evolutionary moralists. — *Presbyterian Review.*

I am particularly obliged to you for Salter's book. Please say to him that I feel that I have gained theoretically as well as practically from reading it. What a noble and pure spirit breathes through the whole! I have derived a fresh confidence in the power of a philosophy of life based on free investigation. — *Professor Harold Höffding, of the University of Copenhagen.*

In the *Zeitschrift für Philosophie und Philosophische Kritik* (*Beigabeheft des* 89 *sten Bandes,* 1886) Professor Jodl says, at the conclusion of an extended review: —

To a book like Strauss's *Old and New Faith* is *Die Religion der Moral* for these reasons infinitely superior, as well with respect to its scientific foundation as to its practical influence; and I cannot omit to recommend Salter's book to the most earnest attention of all those who feel the need of replacing the unhappy dualism between the religious and the scientific stand-points with a comprehensive ideal view.

Sold by all booksellers. Mailed, post-paid, on receipt of price, by the publishers.

ROBERTS BROTHERS, BOSTON.

THE SOURCES OF CONSOLATION IN HUMAN LIFE.

By Rev. WILLIAM R. ALGER,

Author of " The Genius of Solitude," " Friendships of Women," etc.

16mo. Cloth. Price, $1.50.

The writer of this volume, a well-known minister among the Unitarians of New England, having reached nearly threescore years and ten, fittingly takes in hand a topic of special interest to older people and not without attraction even to the young. He is able to speak from experience as well as observation, and to give additional force to what he has to say by having himself seen and known how continually human beings need consolation amid the troubles of life. His purpose here is to furnish a full discussion of the subject and a setting forth of the necessity, the ground, and the essential method of consolation. Nothing doubting that he has something to say which is worth saying, "he hopes to communicate his message in a winsome and effective way, free from the perfunctory quality and mawkish traits so prominent in most books dedicated to this subject."

Mr. Alger arranges the matter of his volume in ten chapters. First, the consolations in human life are classified and illustrated; next, the weeping of humanity in all ages, or "the history of tears," is given. Following this touching chapter comes appropriate and tolerably full considerations of the relation between the calamities of men and the providence of God: the mystery of early deaths, or the mission of the little child; "partings in human life, or the farewells of the world;" "our human need of faith in an all-pervasive and overruling God;" the "true lessons of grief;" the "tragedy of the sea, and its removal;" the "grounds for a cheerful trust in the perfection of divine providence;" "the consolation and true interpretation of the origin, office, and meaning of death;" and in a concluding essay his view of the "latest form of theology, the divine purpose in the universe a perfect consolation for every ill."

These are interesting passages, and they show with what thought and vigor the whole volume is written. The very title of the book will attract attention; and the reader who once opens it will read far into it and, finally, through it. Mr. Alger's style has a pervading charm, and his wide survey of a theme that appeals to the whole human race is made with freshness, force, and originality. — *New York Times.*

Sold by all Booksellers. Mailed, post-paid, by the Publishers,

ROBERTS BROTHERS, BOSTON.

Messrs. Roberts Brothers' Publications.

THY KINGDOM COME.

Ten Sermons on the Lord's Prayer, preached at King's Chapel. By Rev. HENRY WILDER FOOTE.

16mo. Cloth. Price, $1.00.

 A memorial of a beautiful character and a true Christian reaches us in the form of ten of his sermons printed in a neat and handy volume. The late Rev. Henry Wilder Foote was pastor of King's Chapel, Boston. This quaint old stone church — "a rock amid the waves of time" — still stands on Tremont Street. The half-score of discourses are expository of the Lord's Prayer, and have thus a marked unity of thought and style. The volume is entitled "Thy Kingdom Come." Thoughtfulness, deep experience of life, acquaintanceship and communion with spiritual realities, and a fine command of clear and simple language are the characteristics most manifest in these sermons. Mr. Foote had a hatred of mere formalism in words or acts; and loving to tear away the wrapper from the contents of truth, he pressed ever on to the reality within. The sermon on the petition, "Hallowed be Thy name" is a strong example in point, and recalls the power and vividness of Robertson of Brighton. This memorial of a scholar and Christian teacher — one of the brightest ornaments of the Unitarian pulpit — will be welcome to many. — *The Critic.*

 This little volume is one of delightful spiritual reading. It is a book of meditations without a trace of scholastic or polemical theology in it. Its spirit is indicated by such phrases as these, which we gather almost at hazard from its pages: "The first words of this mighty prayer lift us at once to the highest level;" "Names have a deeper connection with things than we sometimes think;" "Christianity has well been called a dispensation of encouragement." These are the meditations of a soul accustomed to live in the higher atmosphere, to think upon the deeper things, and to walk in the sunlight of a great hope and courage. — *Christian Union.*

 The book will not only be treasured highly as a memorial of its author, but the sermons in themselves will be found to be of unusual spiritual power. One hardly needs to be told, as in the few lines of the preface, that these sermons were preached after a time of deep experience. The reader who had not had the privilege of hearing the eminent preacher of King's Chapel will feel, as he reads these living discourses, that it is a rare soul, and one truly enlightened, who speaks to him. The literary character of these sermons is high and chaste, but the helpfulness of the discourses, to souls perplexed about the nature and value of prayer, is their notable characteristic. — *Boston Advertiser.*

Sold by all Booksellers. Mailed, post-paid, by the Publishers,

    ROBERTS BROTHERS, BOSTON.

www.ingramcontent.com/pod-product-compliance
Lightning Source LLC
Chambersburg PA
CBHW021152230426
43667CB00006B/366